OLD STORIES AND CONTEMPORARY ISSUES IN FILMS ABOUT ANTIQUITY AND THE MIDDLE AGES

This volume creates awareness among spectators about the differences between the past and the present, the importance of understanding the past-present relationship, and the reasons behind reconstructions that distort the past in films about Antiquity and the Middle Ages.

Following a historical approach, *Old Stories and Contemporary Issues in Films about Antiquity and the Middle Ages* examines the periods in which films are produced and the eras to which they refer. To show that the absence of a solid historical basis can damage the propagation of good intentions, films that contain political propaganda and stereotypes are examined alongside those that promote tolerance, the condemnation of war and violence, and women's rights. For example, analysis of films such as *Spartacus* (1960) and *300* (2007) reveals a variety of agendas such as the promotion of anachronistic ideals in 1950s America and white supremacist beliefs during the War in Iraq.

Old Stories and Contemporary Issues in Films about Antiquity and the Middle Ages is useful for undergraduates, postgraduates, and scholars interested in the Antiquity and Middle Ages, the relationship between films and History, and modern uses of the past.

Luigi Andrea Berto is Professor of History at Western Michigan University (USA) and teaches classes on pre-modern History and on Film and History. His research focuses on medieval Italy and the Mediterranean, with a special interest in the use and the representation of the past in the modern period.

OLD STORIES AND CONTEMPORARY ISSUES IN FILMS ABOUT ANTIQUITY AND THE MIDDLE AGES

Idealistic Thinking, Sex, Lies, and Video Political Agendas

Luigi Andrea Berto

Routledge
Taylor & Francis Group

LONDON AND NEW YORK

Cover image: 300 HD DVD © Carolyn Jenkins/Alamy Stock Photo

First published 2022
by Routledge
4 Park Square, Milton Park, Abingdon, Oxon OX14 4RN

and by Routledge
605 Third Avenue, New York, NY 10158

Routledge is an imprint of the Taylor & Francis Group, an informa business

© 2022 Luigi Andrea Berto

British Library Cataloguing-in-Publication Data
A catalogue record for this book is available from the British Library

Library of Congress Cataloging-in-Publication Data
A catalog record for this book has been requested

ISBN: 978-0-367-72038-4 (hbk)
ISBN: 978-0-367-72037-7 (pbk)
ISBN: 978-1-003-15313-9 (ebk)

DOI: 10.4324/9781003153139

Typeset in Bembo
by Apex CoVantage, LLC

CONTENTS

FIGURES

MAPS

ACKNOWLEDGMENTS

I wish to thank Laura Pilsworth for accepting this volume for publication, the staff at Routledge, Roberto Pesce, Stefano Trovato, Joe Brandao, Stephanie Falkowski, Hannah Keller, and Matthew Trojacek for their help. Special thanks to Wilson Warren, the historian who believes that historical films are just entertainment.

INTRODUCTION

Thanks to the considerable number of heroic characters and themes that profoundly influenced the development of the Western world, Greco-Roman Antiquity and the Middle Ages have always aroused considerable interest among film directors and spectators alike. Like all movies, unless they are fully subsidized, the main purpose of films based on ancient and medieval plots and characters is to entertain audiences and to make a profit. There is no recipe for a successful movie, but in order not to run the risk of having a work that does not attract a certain number of spectators and does not pay back at least the expenses to produce it, it is necessary (and often not sufficient) to follow more or less the following narrative structure. The protagonist's life, after a normal initial situation, undergoes a drastic change whereby he is forced to face a powerful antagonist. A confrontation between the two follows, usually characterized by twists and turns in which the protagonist suffers defeats, until a new balance is restored, usually with the victory of the protagonist or his ideals. Films based on historical characters and events are not exempted from this formula, as, for example, the limited time available to directors obliges them to create a narrative that viewers can easily understand. The 'rules of the game' for such films are different, and thus history-based movies cannot be judged as one would do with documentaries and even less with academic works.

A skillful mix of images, dialogues, and music can undoubtedly arouse in the audience emotions and interest in the topics dealt with that no academic work can even remotely match. However, it should be noted that when a work of fiction is not limited to set a plot in the past, but refers to specific characters and historical periods, we enter the field of representation of the past, where reality and fiction are so mixed as to be indistinguishable by non-specialists. Although there is a widespread tendency to downplay this problem, proclaiming that a film is not documentary but entertainment, for professional historians and History teachers, this is by no means a negligible issue. They cannot ignore the fact that most people draw

DOI: 10.4324/9781003153139-1

information about the past from movies and that, in order to market their products better, directors and actors often emphasize that their films are historically correct, thus implying that it takes just a couple of hours to learn History. In this way, these filmmakers transgress the 'rules of the game' of fiction and invade the field of History, forgetting, more or less deliberately, that to render their products more understandable and therefore more marketable, they present a past deeply influenced by contemporary issues. These filmmakers must therefore be considered responsible for misunderstandings of History caused by the movies that they have produced.

The aim of this book is neither to condemn historical films nor to reconstruct true History, but rather to create more awareness among students, spectators, and possibly directors and actors about the differences between the past and the present and the importance of understanding the past-present relationship, while, at the same time, grasping the reasons behind reconstructions that distort the past. The book follows a historical approach to films, examining both the period in which they were produced and the era to which they refer. Linguistic and literary theories and film criticism do not fall within the scope of this volume. Besides movies containing political propaganda and stereotypes with racist veins about the 'other', films that propose high ideals such as tolerance, the condemnation of war and violence, and women's rights will also be analyzed, because I am convinced that the absence of a solid historical basis can only damage the propagation of these good intentions.

I do not wish at all to create feelings of guilt among those who liked a movie that I believe to be deeply conditioned by contemporary issues. However, I will consider my goal achieved, if with this book—the reading of which should be combined with the viewing of the films examined here—I succeed in provoking in readers the same reaction provoked in an African-American student of mine after the analysis of a very successful film. Once this student understood that, the fact that the envoys of the 'enemy leader' were always dark-skinned Africans—a historically impossible circumstance because the 'villain' had no dominions in sub-Saharan Africa—indicated that the director had 'unpleasant' ideas about blacks, he approached me after the lecture and told me that, from that moment on, he would watch that movie 'with different eyes.' I also hope that the book will inspire debates like the one that occurred between a student of mine and a fellow student: after attending my lecture on a film about Saint Francis, the former explained to the latter how to see that work that his friend had seen in another course, in which the film had been described as a truthful portrait of Saint Francis.

This book presents several examples but does not claim to have examined all the films on Antiquity and the Middle Ages. Rather, an attempt has been made to analyze movies produced in various parts of the world and in various periods; therefore, both silent films and recent works are considered. Films and TV series based on legends and fictional characters have also been taken into consideration, insofar as they contain topics that are relevant to the analysis conducted in this book. When it is not necessary to quote numerous excerpts and very long texts, the appendices of the chapters will also include translations of the primary sources concerning certain points of the themes mentioned in the films. In this way, the reader will have access to the first indispensable phase of the historian's complex work, the reading of the primary sources.

1

INVADERS AND HEROES

A common theme in films about Antiquity and the Middle Ages is the struggle between evil invaders and a peaceful people who, led by a hero often portrayed as a man forced to take up arms because of the unbearable infamies committed by foreign oppressors, succeeds in driving out the invaders, thus recovering or maintaining its freedom. In the history of cinema, there has been no lack of directors who, sometimes with the help of political organizations or even of states, have used this narrative technique to condemn modern oppressors and invite oppressed of their time to imitate the exemplary behavior of their ancestors.

Let's chase away the Romans, actually the French

In 1924, *Die Hermannschlacht* (*The Battle of Hermann*) by German theater director and playwright Leo König was released. The film recounts the events resulting in one of the worst defeats suffered by the ancient Romans—the Battle of Teutoburg in 9 AD. They fought against some Germanic tribes led by the Cheruschian chief Segimer and his son Arminius. According to Roman historians (the only available ancient sources), the behavior of the Roman general Varus caused that defeat by antagonizing the Germans with his interventions in the fiscal and administrative field. After having collaborated and fought with the Romans, having become a Roman citizen, and having obtained important positions among them, Arminius considered the Romans' behavior to be unbearable and so led their troops into a trap in which most of the soldiers were killed (the general Varus committed suicide not to fall into the hands of the enemies). The episode marked the end of the Romans' expansionism east of the Rhine River. About ninety years after that battle a Roman historian called Arminius the 'liberator of Germany' and wrote that the Germans celebrated him in their songs.

DOI: 10.4324/9781003153139-2

In the fifteenth century, German authors Germanized Arminius' Latin name into Hermann (literally 'army man'), turning him into the savior of their people and glorifying his victory over the Romans as the founding event of Germany's power. In 1875, four years after the coronation of the king of Prussia as emperor of Germany, a ceremony was held to certify the rebirth of German power (the Second Reich). During the ceremony, a huge statue of Arminius was unveiled near the site where the Battle of Teutoburg was believed to have taken place. Significantly, the statue was not facing south, i.e. Rome, but west in the direction of France, modern Germany's worst adversary, which the Prussians had defeated in 1870.

It is no coincidence that the symbolism inherent in that statue was revived during the period in which the film was conceived, produced, and presented to the public. Having defeated Germany in World War I, the victorious nations, particularly France, imposed harsh conditions on the German government that aimed to limit its economic and military power. With this goal and the aim to ensure the payment for the damages suffered in the conflict, the French and the Belgians militarily occupied the most industrialized and rich areas of Germany. The occupation of the Ruhr at the beginning of 1923 caused strong resentment in Germany towards the French and the members of the German center-left government who were considered puppets in the hands of foreigners. The occupation also strengthened the far-right nationalist movements. The situation was exacerbated by French troops' killing of German civilians during various riots, the blocking of economic activities in the Ruhr by the local population, the escalation of conflicts between right and left (in November 1923 Hitler attempted a coup d'état in Munich), and a severe economic crisis with a huge inflation.

In order to have a full understanding of the movie's goal, it must be remembered that the film was probably financed by Hugo Stinnes, an industrialist sympathizer of the nationalist right who played an active role in the fight for the Ruhr and who was among the economic backers of the 'Young German Order', a paramilitary group of the extreme right. It seems that some members of this organization appeared in the film as extras. Although the director's political ideas are unknown, it is likely that he shared those of his sponsor.

The Battle of Hermann contains themes that clearly relate to the situation in Germany in the early 1920s. The nationalists often contrasted the representatives of the government with those who hoped for the rebirth of a strong and independent Germany. The former were portrayed as wily old politicians who only served their own interests and did not oppose the occupation of foreigners whereas the latter were depicted as the new and young forces of the motherland. The film uses a similar technique, depicting a clear generational division between those collaborating with the invaders and those wishing to oppose them. The former are middle-aged persons, while the latter are their children. Arminius's father, Segimer, governs under the dominion of the Romans and his wife favors the invaders to the point of pushing an orphan under her guardianship to be available to the advances of Ventidius, the local Roman commander. The girl, however, loves Sigismund, son of Segestes, who, unlike his father, wants independence from the Romans.

Obviously, there is no reference to the fact that Arminius had collaborated with the Romans and fought at their side. At the beginning of the film, Arminius is in Rome as a hostage and is eager to regain his freedom. The young man loves Tusnelda, the daughter of Segestes, but another Germanic leader, Marobod, promises to ally himself with Segestes under Roman tutelage in exchange for his marriage to Tusnelda. In order to eliminate Arminius, the two devious leaders cowardly attempt to poison him.

Ventidius is portrayed as a perfidious and arrogant man who mercilessly exploits the Germans and does not hesitate to carry out harsh reprisals against those who dare to oppose any of his decisions. The film also references the accusation of having designs on German women that was used to characterize the occupants of the twentieth century. In the film, the Roman commander has a Germanic girl kidnapped to satisfy his carnal desires. Arminius succeeds both in rescuing the Germanic women from the Romans and their Germanic allies and in uniting the hesitant chiefs of his people who elect him their leader. Through such unity, the Germans inflict a crushing defeat on the Romans at whose side Segestes had remained; he is symbolically killed during the battle by his son Sigismund who, equally symbolically, had not recognized his father.

To reinforce the main theme of the film—the liberation of the homeland can only come about through the replacement of the ruling class with young heroes who are the bearers of true Germanic values and the unity of the Germanic people—an instruction booklet accompanied the film. The booklet appealed to patriotism and made reference to Germanic culture by mixing various elements of Scandinavian culture: the god of war Thor, the Norms (mythical creatures charged with controlling the length of men's lives), and the equally mythical Valkyries, immortalized by the famous German musician Richard Wagner (1813–1883) in a very famous opera (many German nationalists adored Wagner and had a considerable fascination with Germanic and Scandinavian myths).

Since many details mentioned in that booklet do not appear in the film, which had a rather low budget and was probably produced quickly as propaganda, and since it could not be assumed that all viewers had read the 'instructions', the premiere of the film, which took place in a small town near the statue of Hermann/Arminius, was preceded by a speech by Paul Warnke, a nationalist intellectual, called 'the poet of the fatherland' by the newspapers that advertised the event. In a packed movie theater, Warnke read a poem—published a few days later in a newspaper—in which he recalled the unity of the Germans and the contemporary situation, comparing quite clearly the ancient Romans to the modern French. After praising Hermann and his fight against the ancient Romans, he added:

> In France's eternal fight against Germany, which is the struggle of lie against truth, of darkness against light, the pure sword will achieve its due victory. Then will come the day of vengeance on which we will push back the enemy from the Saar and Rhine. Then we will break the fetters of slavery and be as German and as free as our Fathers!

The spectators greeted his speech with great enthusiasm. For those who could not benefit from the poet's introduction, the contacts between the past and the present are emphasized immediately after the title of the film with the following prologue.

> In Germany the Roman scourge rules. Arbitrary despotism of a Rome lusting for conquest extended far into Germanic lands. Ruthlessly, the Roman armies of mercenaries savaged [the country], torched and looted with Gallic hatred. Hermann, the son of Cheruscan chief Segimer, is in Roman service as a hostage under the name of Arminius.

The reference to mercenaries and 'Gallic hatred' does not mean that the Romans used troops from Gaul but instead highlights that the modern Gauls, i.e. the French, were present in Germany only for the money.

Various themes dear to the nationalist right, such as the dishonorable behavior of enemies who exploited Germanic women, the freedom of the Germans, the need to find unity to fight the oppression of foreigners, honor, and the sacredness of the homeland, are clearly outlined in a brief dialogue between Arminius and the Roman general Varus.

Arminius: Disgrace upon Rome! It robs a defenseless people and violates their women!
Varus: We are the victors!—We are the power!
Arminius: A united Germany you, Rome, will never subdue!
Varus: You, too, will have to bow to my power!
Arminius: Never!!! We may be defenseless—dishonorable we are not, for ours is
   soil and right!

Another scene in the film emphasizes the need for a strong leader (führer in German) to save Germany by restoring its unity and power. The return of the victorious Arminius is greeted thus: 'Hail Arminius! Savior of Germany!' This need, strongly supported by the right-wing nationalists of those years, became a key component of Hitler's propaganda in Germany's subsequent and much harsher crisis in the early 1930s.

There is also no lack of an invitation to modern German women who, despite the dramatic situation, were to make their contribution to the resistance against foreigners and to preserve the honor of the homeland. As it is typical of periods of strong economic crisis characterized by the occupation of foreign troops, the number of women who prostituted themselves out of necessity was very high and a source of great dishonor for German nationalists when they sold themselves to foreign soldiers. In the film, the scene in which the blonde and beautiful Tusnelda refuses the heavy advances of the Roman commander Ventidius is commented in this way: 'If all women in the country thought like her, the cause of the Germans would be better off.'

It was not only the 'poet of the fatherland' who received the enthusiastic assent of the premiere audience. Numerous scenes met with thunderous applause, and the end of the film was immediately followed by a standing ovation and the singing of the German anthem. In the following days, local and regional newspapers praised the film, emphasizing its points of contact with the contemporary situation. The only newspaper to criticize the movie for its exaggerated nationalism was a newspaper of the Social Democrats, traditional opponents of the right-wing nationalists.

The death of the film's financier a few months after the premiere led to the dissolution of the film company, and this probably led to the non-distribution of *The Battle of Hermann*. The end of the French occupation in 1925 and the advent of sound films also quickly made its viewing unattractive, and the film disappeared from circulation. Fortunately for scholars, a copy—probably confiscated by the Soviets when they conquered a part of Germany in 1945—was discovered in 1990 in Moscow.

The Nazis are coming

Alexander Nevsky (1938) by Soviet director Sergei Eisenstein (1898–1948) is based on the early part of the life of the Prince of Novgorod, Alexander Nevsky (c. 1219–c. 1263), who lived at the time when the territory corresponding to the western part of the Soviet Union of the 1930s was divided into several principalities. He was the son of the Prince of Pereiaslavl and Novgorod, Yaroslav Vsevolodovich, whom he succeeded as prince of Novgorod when his father took control of Kiev in 1236. Shortly thereafter, the Mongols began to invade Russia from the southeast, while the Swedes and the Sword-bearer Knights of Livonia began to press the Novgorod Principality from the west.

Having become Grand Prince of Vladimir, Alexander's father assigned the task of facing the western adversaries to his son Alexander who defeated the Swedes at the mouth of the Neva River (an episode from which his nickname derives). Due to a conflict with the aristocracy of Novgorod, Alexander was forced to leave the city, but was recalled shortly after to face the aggression of the Sword-bearer Knights, whom he defeated on the frozen lake of Peipus in 1241. In the meantime, not being able to face the powerful army of the Mongols, his father recognized their sovereignty over Russia and declared himself their ally. Upon Yaroslav's death in 1246, Alexander succeeded him as prince of Kiev while his brother Andrei had the throne of Vladimir. In 1252, Andrei was expelled because he refused to ally with the new Mongol ruler, and Alexander, favorable to peace with the Mongols, took the title of Grand Prince of Vladimir. Supported by the Orthodox Church, to which the Mongols had granted wide freedom, he continued to follow a policy of cooperation throughout his life, obtaining the gradual exemption from the payment of taxes and the supply of troops to the Mongols. Greatly admired for his skills as a warrior and negotiator, Alexander went down in history as one of the best rulers of Russia and was canonized by the Russian Orthodox Church in Vladimir in 1380 and throughout Russia in 1547.

In the 1920s Eisenstein was the most brilliant representative of Soviet cinema which, unlike the Western cinema whose main objective was the entertainment of the masses, aimed to educate the population according to the principles of Communism. Like all arts, cinema could not be apolitical. In line with these ideas, Eisenstein directed films that extolled the struggles of Communists against the oppression of the Tsarist regime.

Following the intellectual principles in vogue among Soviet filmmakers of those years, he did not shoot them following a simple plot. Instead, he used a theoretical approach aimed at arousing emotional shocks in viewers. To learn the techniques of sound films Eisenstein spent several years abroad (mainly in Hollywood) and when he returned in 1932, he discovered a Soviet Union very different from the one he had known. Stalin had in fact taken full control of power and had begun to eliminate all those who opposed his plans to centralize power and complete the collectivization of the society. The arts were not immune to the new atmosphere. They had to be devoid of any sophisticated intellectual elaboration and follow the principles of real Socialism. For cinema, this meant that movies had to use a very simple plot. Following Stalin's directives of 'Socialism in one nation' and the exaltation of the 'great man', in Soviet films of the 1930s the pre-revolutionary history of Mother Russia, characterized by powerful and heroic 'fathers', replaced both the stories about the revolutionary struggles of the twentieth century and the egalitarianism and internationalism of the 1920s.

Eisenstein struggled to adapt to the new climate, but realized that in addition to his career, he risked losing his life when one of his projects was cancelled by the director of the Soviet film agency in March 1937. Eisenstein condemned that film in front of a commission, pointing out his mistakes, and declared that his next work would follow the directives of the Communist Party and would be completely devoid of his previous misconceptions.

> There is only one possible subject for my next work: spiritually heroic, following the Party's ideology, treating of war and defense, and popular in style. . . . In preparation for the making of this film, I see the path through which I shall obliterate the last traces of elemental anarchy from my world view and my creative method.

Considering that just then a very dangerous threat to the Soviet Union, namely Nazi Germany, was rising in the West, the deeds of an ancient Russian hero like Alexander Nevsky, the savior of his homeland from the 'Germans of the Middle Ages', were a perfect subject for the director eager to continue working (and surviving) in the new Soviet Union. To ensure that Eisenstein followed the new party line, the director was surrounded by spies; a favorite of Stalin's was appointed as his co-director, and a Secret Service agent was assigned as his co-scriptwriter. A member of the Supreme Soviet played the main role.

To avoid any misunderstanding, in an article published in conjunction with the release of the film, Eisenstein proved to be in line with the values of the Communist Party, pointing out that he had directed a film that corresponded to what was expected of an artistic work in the Soviet Union and that showed exemplary behavior and a lesson of the past to be imitated in the present.

> The theme of patriotism and natural defense against the aggressor is the subject that suffuses our film. We have taken an historical episode from the thirteenth century, when the ancestors of today's Fascists, the Teutonic and Livonian knights, waged a systematic struggle to conquer and invade the East in order to subjugate the Slav and other nationalities in precisely the same spirit that Fascist Germany is trying to do so, with the same frenzied slogans and the same fanaticism.

In the film, the Sword-bearer Knights (always referred to as 'knights' or 'Germans') are portrayed as the equivalent of modern Germans suspected of wanting to expand into Eastern Europe just as that military order had done in the Middle Ages. To make this connection more explicit, the heraldic emblem on the helmet of one of the knights depicts a hand pointing upwards, a gesture similar to that of the Nazi salute (image 1.1). Moreover, the Catholic bishop present among the ranks of the invaders wears gloves and a miter marked with a symbol similar to the swastika, the emblem par excellence of the Nazis (image 1.2). In a 1939 article, the director himself pointed out that there was no difference between what the knights had committed in the Middle Ages and what was happening in Europe.

> When you read the chronicles of the thirteenth century alternately with current newspapers, you lose your sense of difference in time, because the bloody terror which the conquering Orders of Knighthood sowed is scarcely distinguishable from what is now being perpetrated in Europe.

FIGURE 1.1   Helmet with Nazi salute (screenshot from *Alexander Nevsky*)

FIGURE 1.2 Bishop with swastika (screenshot from *Alexander Nevsky*)

Other scenes in the film depict a compact rank of knights who massacre the defenseless population of the city of Pskov and infantrymen who snatch children from their mothers' arms and throw them into the fire (images 1.3, 1.4). Such scenes evoke the violence that took place in Europe shortly before the film was released (for example, the bombing of the Spanish city of Guernica by the German air force in April 1937) and constitute a warning to the Soviets that they could be the next victims of the Nazis.

In another scene, a bishop among the knights justifies their invasion by stating that there is only one Rome. This sentence seems to suggest that this military order legitimized its aggression against the Slavs because the only true Christianity was the Catholic one, i.e. that of Rome, and therefore it was legitimate to attack the Slavs who, being Orthodox Christians, did not follow the true Christian religion. Since the bishop, however, does not speak of Catholics and Orthodox, but of Rome, those words can also refer to a broader issue. Following the Ottoman conquest of Constantinople in 1453—considered the second Rome by the Byzantines for whom the first Rome had disappeared with the deposition of the last Western Roman emperor in 476—the Russians proclaimed that Moscow was the third Rome. This was denied by the Catholics, who instead claimed that the heir of ancient Rome was the Catholic Church led by the bishop of Rome, the pope. This religious and ideological diatribe, obviously anachronistic for the thirteenth century when the 'second Rome' still existed and Moscow was not the head of a

FIGURE 1.3   German foot soldiers (screenshot from *Alexander Nevsky*)

FIGURE 1.4   Burning of Russian babies (screenshot from *Alexander Nevsky*)

Russian state, concerned, at least officially, the Orthodox Christian world of Eastern Europe before the creation of the atheistic Soviet Union. However, it was still useful for the Communist regime because it gave an ideological coloring to the aggressors that could be easily understood by the Russians for whom Orthodox Christianity still had a strong identity value.

In those years, Rome was also the capital of Fascist Italy which was allied to the Nazis and considered a formidable enemy by the Soviets. Although not obvious to normal spectators, Eisenstein declared in an essay on the film that the battle between Nevsky's army and the German cavalrymen was inspired by the battle of Cannae where the Romans were defeated by the Carthaginian general Hannibal, the most formidable adversary of ancient Rome whose splendor Mussolini wanted to recreate. The essay suggests that Eisenstein had this connection between Italy and the Nazis in mind.

In addition to the external enemies, Alexander Nevsky and his supporters must also face the internal ones, the orthodox churchman Ananias and especially the merchant Tverdilo, who symbolize the adversaries the Soviet Union had to deal with, namely the orthodox clergymen and the advocates of private property and free trade. Following the image created by Soviet propaganda for their twentieth-century counterparts, they act in three ways: directing public opinion toward decisions favorable to them, providing military information to external enemies, and after the outbreak of hostilities, siding with them.

Ananias and Tverdilo try to persuade the inhabitants of Novgorod not to take up arms against the Germans and to agree to be subordinate to them; they help the invaders to conquer Pskov and give them information about the movements of Alexander's troops, causing them serious losses. During the final battle, Tverdilo sides with the Germans, cowardly hiding his face, and when he is discovered, kills a heroic inhabitant of Novgorod. The manner in which Tverdilo is punished for his treason evokes the rhetoric of popular justice against spies and internal enemies created in the Soviet Union, where the request for the death sentence of supposed traitors came from a crowd that was paraded through the streets of cities under police control. In the film, Nevsky asks the population of Pskov to determine what punishment Tverdilo deserves. He is immediately killed by the crowd (in reality, the leader of Pskov was assassinated for opposing Nevsky's policy of compromise toward the Mongols).

In order not to compromise the image of the all-in-one hero and at the same time conform to the official Soviet line of the 'great man', the director falsifies historical reality and shows that Alexander proves to be neither servile nor complacent towards the Mongols and refuses the Mongols' offer to join them. The scenes of the famous battle on the ice in which Alexander fights in the front line and defeats and captures the enemy commander were also invented to highlight the courage and valor of the prince.

The hero of the film and his supporters are also explicitly presented as champions and defenders of the Russian motherland. This theme appears from the very beginning of the film when, while Alexander and his men are fishing in a lake, they

FIGURE 1.5   Alexander Nevsky among his soldiers (screenshot from *Alexander Nevsky*)

sing a song in which they say that they fought against the Swedes for 'Great Mother Russia.' To the emissaries of Novogorod who invite him to defend their city, the prince replies that he will avenge the sufferings of Russia. In an earlier scene, he defines Novgorod as 'the last stand for Russia', and at the end of the film he says:

> Go and tell all in alien lands that Rus lives . . . he who comes to us sword in hand by the sword will perish. On that our Russian land will forever take its stand!

In this regard, the clash of opinions between the inhabitants of Novgorod who wanted to come to an agreement with the Germans (the already mentioned Ananias and Tverdilo) and those wishing to fight them reflects the profound difference between those who were true Russians, i.e. those who cared about the homeland and the common good, and those for whom the homeland meant nothing and thought only of their own material interests. To the latter, who said that the cities invaded by the enemies meant nothing to them and that they would give the Germans some of their many goods, if necessary, the former replied that, for people like Ananias and Tverdilo, having a mother or a stepmother is the same thing and that they wanted to trade Russia for goods.

Aware that some might consider the ideas of 'Russia' and 'the homeland' anachronistic for the thirteenth century, the director cleverly makes the traitors say, 'What Russia? Where have you seen it last?' and 'Wherever you make your bed, there's your homeland.' However, the supporters of the second option succeed in prevailing, proving that although physically a united Russia did not exist at that time, it was already present as an ideal. The director thus proved to be in line with the directives of the government of the Soviet Union. The absence of sources contemporary to the real Alexander Nevsky prevents us from establishing with certainty whether those ideals already existed (Eisenstein chose that character precisely because it allowed him not to be conditioned by historical reality). Still, from what is known about the prince, it is evident that he acted to preserve power and perhaps to do so he used those ideas.

The director shows that the hero is engaged both in preparing the plan for the final battle and in fighting on the front line with his men, thus alluding to the fact that Stalin too would have been ready to lead the Russians in the new struggle against the Germans. To leave no room for doubt, Eisenstein clarified this detail in an article in a widely circulated newspaper while he was shooting the film.

> For if the might of our national soul was able to punish the enemy in this way, when the country lay exhausted in the grip of the Tatar [Mongol] yoke, then nothing will be strong enough to destroy this country which has broken the last chains of its oppression; a country which has become a Socialist motherland; a country which is being led to unprecedented victories by the greatest strategist in world history—Stalin.

At the end of the film, Alexander reminds his subjects not to forget what has just happened and tells them that, in case of danger, he would call all of Russia to fight the enemies and would punish those who did not respond. His children would do the same thing after his death. The director likely intended Stalin to represent one of the sons of Alexander, and it is likely that the Soviet audience viewed Stalin this way.

Stalin also wished to project a reassuring and peaceful image and loved to present himself as a father of the people. To reinforce this image, he was often depicted with children in his arms. It is therefore no coincidence that at the end of the film the victorious prince is portrayed precisely in that manner. In his autobiography, Eisenstein relates that in the original script, the film ends with the prince being poisoned after submitting to the Mongols in order to gain time. However, this part was criticized by Soviet censors, and someone deleted it (with a red pen, the comment that 'such a great prince could not die' was added).

However powerful this 'great man' was, he was not a comic book superhero and so could not do everything by himself. According to Soviet rhetoric, the support of the proletarians was essential to this great man's rule. Unlike the real Nevsky's army, composed of professional warriors, in the film Alexander is asked to lead an army of peasants (the proletarians of the Middle Ages) against the German invaders. Demonstrating a great collective spirit, worthy of the inhabitants of the Soviet Union (at least according to the propaganda of that state), the artisans (the workers of the Middle Ages) of Novgorod agree to provide free weapons for that army. Among them there is also a champion of collectivization, the armorer Ignat, who donates his armor and all his weapons, leaving for himself only a tiny iron mesh that cannot protect him from the enemies' blows during the battle.

Alexander Nevsky rehabilitated Eisenstein in the eyes of the Soviet authorities. He was awarded several prestigious prizes and honors and received the approval of Stalin, who at the premiere of the film shook the director's hand and patted him on the shoulder, saying 'Sergei Mikhailovic, you are a good Bolshevik after all!', a comment that underlines the mortal danger the director faced (since he died nine years later at the age of fifty, the stress of that period probably shortened his life).

The film was so intimately connected to the period in which it was produced that its life in movie theaters depended on the rapid changes in the international scenario. Not even a year after its release, one of its main messages, the terrible depiction of the Germans in the Middle Ages, had become extremely embarrassing for the Soviet government who, in order to share Poland with Germany, had signed a non-aggression pact with the Germans in August 1939. *Alexander Nevsky* was therefore withdrawn from movie theaters and the anti-Nazi propaganda immediately ceased. In December 1939, Eisenstein was even asked to direct one of the most representative German operas, *Die Walkurie* by Wagner, in the most famous theater in Moscow, the Bolshoi. This initiative aimed 'to bring Germanic and Norse epic closer to us.' In June 1941 Germany attacked the Soviet Union and the film returned to Soviet movie theaters. Shortly after the death of the Soviet dictator in 1953, a destalinization campaign began in the Soviet Union. Consequently, *Alexander Nevsky* was shown less and less.

The theme of the Germans invading the Slavic world during the Middle Ages resurfaced during the Cold War in a film produced in Poland, another eastern European nation ruled by a Communist regime and an ally of the Soviet Union. *Krzyzacy* (1960), or *Knights of the Teutonic Order* in English, directed by the most important Polish director of those years, Alexandr Ford, is set in the period of the battle of Tannenberg/Grünwald (July 1410) between the military order of the Teutonic Knights and the King of Poland and Lithuania, Jogaila (known by the Poles as Wladislaw II). The film narrates the story of a young Lithuanian nobleman, Zbyszko, who is in love with Danusia, daughter of the Polish nobleman, Jurand. When the latter defends some Polish merchants who were captured by the Teutonic Knights, the knights take revenge by mutilating the Polish aristocrat, killing his wife, and kidnapping his daughter, who, having gone crazy during captivity, dies shortly after being freed by Zbyszko. The latter then falls in love with a childhood friend, Jagna, daughter of a neighbor of his uncle. The film ends with the battle of Tannenberg.

Poland was the first victim of the military expansionism of Nazi Germany, under whose harsh domination it remained for almost the entirety of World War II. Ford's decision not to make a film set during that conflict or aimed at telling an epic story strongly characterized by propaganda tones as in *Alexander Nevsky* was probably linked to his desire to concentrate above all on the long history of the cruel behavior of the Germans towards the Poles and the other populations of Eastern Europe.

The terrible violence inflicted on the inhabitants, the tremendous exploitation to which they were subjected, and the severe damage caused to their lands by the Nazis was nothing new. The Teutonic Knights of the fifteenth century had behaved like the Germans in World War II. In fact, although the film shows some episodes that demonstrate the typical behavior of the Teutonic Knights, such episodes recalled events that had taken place about twenty years before the film was made. As already mentioned, they carry out a terrible reprisal against Jurand and his family. Jurand's journey to the castle of the Teutonic Knights takes place in a desolate landscape dotted with gallows of people hanged for not having paid taxes (including women and children). Some of the subjects are forced to make weapons under the threat of the guards' whips. There is also a reference to the degenerate, disrespectful, and vain behavior of the warrior monks who talk to King Jogaila's envoys in the main hall of their castle while drinking and eating in abundance and sporting peacock feathers on their helmets. Additionally, the serious conversations between them and the guests are constantly interrupted by the jokes of jesters.

Unlike Eisenstein, Ford was not pressured by an asphyxiating present (the looming Nazi threat and the orders of the Soviet apparatus) and could therefore afford to add some nuances in his description of the Teutonic Knights, which allowed him to emphasize the wickedness of the bad knights, who constituted the majority of the Teutonics. The elderly and soon-to-be-dead Grand Master of the Teutonic Knights is portrayed as a mediator between the various instances and, shortly before his death, calls on the knights to keep peace with the Poles and the Lithuanians. It should be noted that this depiction is in line with the one made by a chronicler fifty years after the death of that historical figure. In the film, one of the Teutonic Knights also tries to prevent the kidnapping of Danusia and is therefore wounded with a shot in the back. He later testified against that crime in front of King Jogaila.

To highlight the aggressive spirit of the Germans further and to exalt the success of their opponents, Ford distorts history by showing that the battle of Tannenberg occurred because the Teutonics refused the peace offer of King Jogaila, who went to them in a last attempt at conciliation, and that the Polish king's victory was decisive. In reality, the clash was the product of the Poles' and Lithuanians' offensive against the Teutonic Knights in response to the continuous raids of the warrior monks in Lithuania. The knights' defeat put an end to their aims in Lithuania, but they still managed to preserve most of their possessions. To non-specialists, the composition of the coalition that clashed with the Teutonics in Tannenberg may seem anachronistic and a tribute to the modern composition of the Warsaw Pact since, along with the Lithuanians and Poles, there are also Russian and Tartar warriors and a Czech (a friend of Zbyszko). In reality, the director did his job quite well. Among the ranks of the fifteenth-century army there were in fact mercenaries from areas corresponding to the modern Czech Republic and Romania (and perhaps even from Russia) and Tartars.

Probably influenced by Poland's spirit of autonomy at the end of the 1950s, Ford avoided the propagandistic excesses present in *Alexandr Nevsky*. Unlike the latter movie, his film portrays the Polish merchants as victims of, not collaborators with, the enemy; nobles and common people do not mix. Jogaila's army is made up of professional warriors, not peasants, and the sovereign does not fight in the front line. More realistically, he leads his troops from the rear. Noteworthy is the absence of any criticism against Polish churchmen who had always played a crucial role in maintaining Polish identity (even during the Cold War). The German monk saved by Zbyszko from a snowstorm is, not surprisingly, portrayed as a sympathetic trickster who helps the Lithuanians free Danusia.

Italians before the nation

In February 1503, in the midst of Italy's division into various states and a war between France and Spain for the control of the South of the Peninsula, a sort of duel took place between thirteen French knights and thirteen Italian knights in the service of Spain. The clash began when a French officer remarked upon the cowardice of the Italian soldiers. Led by Ettore Fieramosca, the Italians defeated the French. In the following centuries this episode, known as the 'Challenge of Barletta', became a symbol of Italian courage and of their indomitable spirit that they showed in adverse conditions and in response to the arrogance of foreign invaders even before the formation of the Italian nation. The episode was celebrated in various literary works and monuments and, after the formation of the Italian state in the second half of the nineteenth century, was mentioned in the textbooks of Italian schools up until a few years ago. For Italians, it was (and, although it has lost some of its luster, it still is) such a famous event and was so imbued with positive values that it could not fail to be represented in some movies. The periods in which those films were produced are significant because they coincide with years in which the exaltation of Italian patriotism and the greatness of Italy was particularly heated.

The first film dates to 1909 at a time we will discuss when we examine *The Ship* in Chapter 4. The second was released in 1915—at the beginning of World War I when Italy wanted to acquire the areas of the Peninsula still under foreign rule. The third appeared in 1938 when the Italian Fascist regime was trying to transform the country into a world power. In the case of Alessandro Blasetti's 1938 film *Ettore Fieramosca*, however, it is misleading to consider it a regime film permeated with Fascist propaganda. Most of Blasetti's work in fact centers on the events preceding the famous duel and portrays the heroic behavior of Fieramosca and his tormented love story with a noblewoman.

Obviously, there are references to the honor of the Italians, to the duty of defending it, and to the arrogance of the French invaders, which is opposed to the honorable behavior of the Spaniards, who despite being invaders themselves, are portrayed in a very sympathetic way. Undoubtedly, these particularities corresponded perfectly with the situation in which the film was released. In those years, a civil war was, in fact, taking place in Spain. Italy intervened by sending logistical support and volunteers to help the Spaniards who had rebelled against the legitimate Republican government. In the 1930s, the French republican government symbolized the enemy par excellence of the Italian dictatorship and consequently many opponents of the Fascist regime had taken refuge in France. In order to

obtain permission to make the film, which was denied in 1935, Blasetti emphasized the themes that would characterize the work and that were dear to the Fascist
regime. The director pointed out that it was necessary to make a 'movie that effectively talks about Fascist Italy to 50 million foreigners.' However, these themes are
only hinted at in his work. Probably because it was not a one-way film and could
therefore satisfy the tastes of various types of viewers, *Ettore Fieramosca* was a great
success with the public.

China and the new Silk Road

Tiān Jiàng Xióng Shī (*Celestial General, Heroic Army*), also known as *Dragon Blade*, is a
2015 film produced in China and the United States that, although a work of complete fantasy, deserves to be examined in this book, because it mentions the ancient
Romans and expresses a number of messages clearly influenced by the international
situation in the second decade of the third millennium. The film tells the story of
Huo An, a Chinese officer who heads a special team with the task of protecting
the Silk Road, the network of trade routes that connected China to the Mediterranean, and preventing conflicts among the peoples living along that route. After
having faced the Roman general Lucius in a duel (ending in a draw), Huo An and
his men fraternize with Lucius's legionaries and, together with them, battle a huge
Roman army led by Lucius's opponent, the evil Tiberius. Just when all the good
Romans, most of Huo An's men, and their Asian allies have been killed by the evil
Romans, a huge army of Parthians (ancient inhabitants of an area roughly corresponding to modern Iran) arrives and defeats the villains (the supervillain Tiberius
is killed by the Chinese hero).

The film is an obvious call for a peacemaker in Asia and a mediator between
Asia and the West, styling China as the one able to fulfill such a role in the contemporary world. According to the Chinese government, this objective would bring
peace and prosperity, but in order to succeed, it needs the community of intent of
the Asian peoples and the free circulation of goods in the world (under the supervi-
sion of China) which in the third millennium could be achieved by creating a new
Silk Road comparable to the ancient one. The project is feasible with the support
of the good Romans, i.e. the good Westerners and in particular good Americans,
willing, unlike the bad ones, to cooperate and prosper together with the Chinese.
Worthy of note is that the film also shows the great results that can be obtained by
combining the technological knowledge of the Romans with the industriousness
of the Chinese. The latter, of course, possess moral qualities and an educational system superior to that of the good Romans. To Lucius, who remarks that in Rome
he was taught to kill, Huo An replies that in China he was taught to make peace.

Not surprisingly, the film was a great commercial success in China, while abroad
it was received very tepidly and seen only as an action film. Noteworthy is the
criticism from the media in India, the traditional opponent of Chinese expansionism in Southwest Asia, which were quick to point out the propagandistic aspects
of the film.

2

INSPIRING MODELS OF UNITY, INDEPENDENCE, AND IDENTITY

Films based on the struggle between evil invaders and a peaceful people, led by a hero, were used to invite contemporary viewers to imitate the exemplary behavior of their ancestors, but sometimes had an additional purpose. Indeed, movies with such a theme were used to demonstrate ancient origins of peoples, even if they had formed their own state only in modern times, thereby strengthening the legitimacy of the existence of that state. Some of those films were also utilized to legitimize the demands for independence of the inhabitants of some parts of contemporary Europe who felt that their past indicated that they had the right to create their own state.

The ancient and medieval origins of Romania and the Romanians

For a few short periods between the first century BC and the first century AD, the Dacians had managed to create a powerful kingdom in an area partly corresponding to modern Romania, a so-called new nation formed by the union of several principalities in the second half of the nineteenth century. In order to cement that union, the ancient Dacians were used as the founding moment of the Romanian people and nation. As indicated by the name of the new nation (Romania = the land of the Romans), the ancient Romans, who had subjugated the Dacians, played a role in shaping modern Romania. Although the Romans had put an end to the independence of the Dacians and had resided in the territory corresponding to modern Romania only for about one hundred and seventy years (106–271 AD), it was argued that the people born from the union between the Roman conquerors and the conquered Dacians had taken on the best qualities of both peoples. The Roman conquest had also incorporated the peoples of Dacia into Western civilization. Thanks to this incorporation, this people retained its identity over the centuries, even if it was subjugated by foreign powers.

DOI: 10.4324/9781003153139-3

Such narrative was maintained even after World War II when the Communists took control of Romania. Indeed, this idea found new vigor in the 1960s when Romania began to take positions not in line with those of the Soviet Union (this trend developed especially with Nicolae Ceaușescu, who became head of the Communist Party in 1965 and was head of state from 1967 until his violent elimination in 1989). Having explained the cultural and political context in which the films were produced, it is now appropriate to present a summary of the main events concerning the achievement of unity of the peoples of ancient Dacia and the interactions they had with the Romans.

In the middle of the first century BC, the Dacian leader Burebista succeeded in uniting all the peoples of Dacia into a single kingdom for the first time. Having occupied Macedonia, the Romans believed that the creation of that powerful state on the borders of their domains was a threat to their interests in the area south of the Danube. Taking advantage of the call for help from the Greek cities on the west coast of the Black Sea that had been occupied by the Romans, Burebista attacked them and extended his kingdom into the area surrounding the Danube delta. He then tried to take advantage of the civil war among the Romans by siding with Pompey against Caesar in 48 BC, who defeated and eliminated his opponent. However, the assassination of Caesar in 44 BC saved Burebista from the punitive expedition of the Roman dictator. Yet shortly afterwards, the Dacian ruler fell victim to a conspiracy.

His disappearance ended the unity of the peoples of Dacia until one hundred and twenty years later when it was reunited under Duras-Diurpaneus. In 85 AD, his army made an incursion south of the Danube into the Roman province of Moesia, sacking the region and defeating the Romans. This provoked the reaction of the Romans who, led by Emperor Domitian, pushed the Dacians back north of the Danube and advanced in Dacia. But the Romans were defeated in 86. Two years later, however, the Romans were again victorious over the Dacians who were under the command of Decebalus. Engaged by both internal and external enemies, Domitian preferred to make peace with Decebalus. The situation changed with Emperor Trajan (98–117), who wanted to eliminate that powerful adversary and to take possession of Dacia's rich gold mines. After two tough campaigns, the Romans managed to achieve a decisive victory against the Dacians. Rather than falling into the hands of the enemies, Decebalus preferred to commit suicide. Dacia became a Roman province and many subjects of the Roman Empire settled there.

Dacii (1967) by Sergiu Nicolaescu is set in the first Roman attempt to conquer Dacia in 87–88 AD and clearly aims to glorify the heroic behavior of the Dacians against the invaders. Yet at the same time, the film also alludes to the fact that modern Romanians stem from the union of the two best representatives of the Dacians and the Romans. Given this connection, it is noteworthy that the movie emphasizes that the best Roman was already the product of the union between the two peoples. The plot summary highlights these aspects well.

The film begins with the Roman army ready to cross the Danube to invade Dacia. The Roman general Fuscus plots to eliminate Emperor Domitian who has just arrived to lead the campaign against the Dacians. Upon hearing that another population is threatening the borders of the Roman empire, Domitian decides to enter into an agreement with the Dacians so that he can use his army against that powerful enemy. Attius and his son Severus are sent to parliament with the Dacians, but as soon as they enter their territory, a Dacian scout kills Attius. Domitian then orders to attack. In the meantime, the King of the Dacians, Decebalus, knowing of the death of Attius, reveals that he was not a Roman, but a Dacian sent to Rome many years before to promote the interests of his compatriots and to keep them informed of the Romans' plans.

The Dacians prepare themselves for the clash and, following their traditions, they sacrifice their best warrior, the son of Decebalus, to the gods. The young man willingly accepts the sacrifice. The Dacians then eliminate the vanguard of the Roman troops commanded by Severus, who is wounded in the clash, but the daughter of Decebalus, Meda, finds him and heals him. The two fall in love and Decebalus accepts that union and asks Severus to convince Domitian to make peace. Severus, however, replies that he must do his duty as a Roman officer and the Dacian king lets him return to the Romans. Discovering that General Fuscus wants to kill the emperor, Severus refuses to help him and kills him in a duel. Domitian is informed of everything and orders Severus to attack Decebalus who confronts and kills him. Before dying, the Roman officer says to the Dacian sovereign: 'This is all I could do for you.' The film then ends with the two armies clashing. Thanks to the director, who knew how to mix themes dear to Romanian patriotism and in tune with the Romanian political line of those years, *Dacii* had a remarkable success with the public and became one of the most seen Romanian films.

More complex was *Columna* (1968) by Mircea Drăgan that completed the history of the encounters between Dacians and Romans because this film treated the delicate theme of how the Roman conquest of Dacia had occurred and how the interactions between the two peoples had taken place. The movie takes its title from the so-called Column of Trajan in whose reliefs are described the various stages of Dacia's Roman conquest and the Romanization of that area.

The film begins with the end of the wars to take possession of that area and is set in the period of transformation of a part of the Dacian kingdom into a Roman province. Although the Romans are the winners, they are not portrayed as ruthless exploiters. On the contrary, they prove willing to collaborate with the natives to create a fruitful union between the two peoples in the spirit of mutual respect. In this way, the filmmaker tried to reduce the brutal aspects of the conquest and invited to look to the future. Notably, in the scene in which the head of Decebalus is presented to the emperor, only the sack that contains it is shown. The Roman general Tiberius, who defeated Decebalus, is appointed governor of Dacia and succeeds in obtaining the collaboration of the Dacians by showing clemency toward them. He also proves to have no preconceptions about the conquered and, after having forgiven a Dacian noblewoman named Andrada for having killed a Roman, he falls in love with her and manages to conquer her with his love. From their marriage a son is born, a symbol of the synthesis between the two peoples, and his birth is significantly celebrated by both Romans and Dacians. Tiberius is also willing to use the technological knowledge of the Romans to improve the lives of the Dacians. Another Roman ready to collaborate and bond with the locals is the centurion Sabinus who marries a Dacian priestess. When he goes blind following a clash with Dacian rebels, Sabinus becomes a school master and teaches Roman culture to Dacian children. Dacian culture is, however, not obliterated by the conquerors and Andrada teaches her son the traditions of her people.

The process of synthesis between the two peoples is, nevertheless, complex. In fact, on one hand, the film highlights the Dacians' great valor, while on the other, it recognizes the several obstacles on the long path towards the benefits the Dacians could gain by working with the Romans. To point out that the success of the Romans was not just a result of their power and technological superiority, the movie uses the theme of the internal traitor, a characteristic element of the nationalistic narrative of Romanian history and one that is present in other historical films characterized by the dialectic invaders and heroes. The heroes, the defenders of the Romanian people, are killed because of the internal traitors. Bastus on whom the Dacians placed their trust reveals the weaknesses of the Dacians' defenses to Trajan, leading to their defeat and Decebalus's death. The traitor is then captured by the Dacians and judged by the people.

After the demise of Decebalus, not all Dacians are willing to accept the Roman domination and a group of them, led by the faithful collaborator of Decebalus, Gerula, continues the fight with a group of Dacians. Among them is the grandson of Decebalus whom Gerula hopes to make the king of the resurrected Dacian kingdom. When the grandson of Decebalus becomes an adult, Gerula believes that it is time to attack, and during the offensive they kill some of the Dacians who had chosen to collaborate with the Romans.

Tiberius tries to mediate and make it clear that continued fighting will weaken both the Dacians and the Romans and will allow fierce foreign peoples to invade them. In talking to Tiberius's son, Gerula understands that the Dacian heritage is alive in him and that he represents the product of the synthesis between Dacians and Romans. The leader of a northern population proposes that Gerula and his men unite with him to drive out the Romans. Gerula, however, knows that such an alliance would replace the new masters, who brought civilization with other masters who would bring barbarism, and therefore convinces Decebalus's grandson to help the Romans. The barbarians attack but are defeated by the Dacian–Roman collaboration. However, since the old generation is still too tied to the past, it must disappear. After Decebalus's grandson dies on the battlefield, Gerula sees Tiberius approaching his body and mistakenly thinks that the Roman wants to behead him as he had done with Decebalus. So, he kills him. When he realizes his mistake, he tells Tiberius's son that he must follow his father's example as a great warrior who fought for his people and defend the new nation his father created. As you can see, *Columna* has a much more complex plot than *Dacii* and deals with the extremely delicate topic of the Dacian-Roman synthesis. However, these were topics that had always characterized Romanian patriotism; therefore, even if to a lesser degree than *Dacii*, *Columna* was well received by the Romanian public.

In 1980, the ancient history of Romania was again the subject of a film, *Burebista* by Georghe Vitanidis. Unlike *Dacii* and *Columna*, which had followed the patriotic narrative established with the creation of modern Romania and had not been influenced by the Communist government, that movie was instead commissioned by Ceauşescu, who had strongly accentuated the authoritarian aspects of his government and had developed a cult of personality, presenting himself as the strong man necessary for Romania to maintain its autonomy and identity within the bloc of Communist nations in Central and Eastern Europe. Consequently, this film moved away from the Romanian patriotic tradition, which emphasized the greatness of the synthesis between Dacians and Romans, and instead constructed a new narrative in which the birth of the Romanian nation was attributed to a strong and paternal leader whose authoritarian features were necessary to create and maintain the unity of its people.

It is noteworthy that the film focuses on a character and a period about which, because of the scarcity of sources, very little was known or only known by a few specialists. The character and the period could therefore be shaped at will. This particularity becomes clear when one considers that the purpose of the film was to celebrate the supposed two thousand and fiftieth anniversary of the unification of the nation that would become Romania. Although the unity of Dacian people had in fact been transitory and Burebista was eventually eliminated by a Dacian plot, the filmmaker resolves this dilemma at the end of the film with Burebista's remark that rulers may die but what they had accomplished—the unity of the nation—would last forever.

Not only does the Roman component in the creation of Romania disappear, but the Romans assume the role of perfidious aggressors eager to end the freedom of the Dacians. Moreover, Burebista, a clear nod to Ceauşescu, emerges as a shining example not only for the Dacians/Romanians, but also for all those who wanted to defend the freedom of men from an oppressive regime. In fact, Burebista is presented as a sort of continuer of Spartacus's feat, the gladiator who, with his revolt, had brought freedom and dignity to thousands of slaves and had made the mighty Rome tremble. A young man who had fought with Spartacus and who was later revealed to be Burebista's son took refuge with the Dacian leader and explained to him who Spartacus was.

Just as Ceauşescu wanted to highlight his role as a Communist leader who acted autonomously from the Soviet Union and who refused to go along with its aggressive policies within the Communist bloc (he had not, for example, sided with the Soviet intervention in Czechoslovakia in 1968), the Burebista of the film is presented as a wise leader who had tried to convince the peoples not subjugated by Rome to maintain peace among themselves. Significantly, Burebista's wisdom is contrasted with the fanaticism of a leader of a Celtic tribe who refuses to establish a peaceful agreement with the Dacians and does not hesitate to plunder Dacia.

Despite the epic tone and the exemplarity of the protagonist, *Burebista* was too far removed from the patriotic narrative that had distinguished modern Romania, and therefore its success was not as comparable to that of *Dacii* and *Columna*. With the bloody elimination of Ceaușescu in 1989, the Romanian people tried to forget that film so connected to that dictator. Nowadays, however, *Burebista* is appreciated by the Romanians who, being born after the Ceaușescu era and not knowing the context in which that film was produced, prefer to see an autochthonous origin of their nation.

In the 1970s, the films about the Dacians and the Roman conquest of Dacia were not the only historical films to deal with the origins of the Romanians and their country. In fact, three such movies set in the medieval and early modern periods were produced between the release of *Dacii* and *Burebista*. The late Middle Ages and the first part of the early modern age are especially relevant for the history of the area that would become modern Romania. In the Middle Ages, the region corresponding to Transylvania was under the control of the kings of Hungary who, between the twelfth and thirteenth centuries, granted favorable conditions to Germans and Hungarians to settle in that territory. They could have considerable autonomy while being governed by an official appointed by the king of Hungary. Taking advantage of various dynastic crises and internal problems in Hungary, the inhabitants of Transylvania organized various revolts which were however always repressed. While remaining under Hungarian rule, the Transylvanians managed to obtain various privileges and prosper.

The other two main areas of modern Romania, Wallachia and Moldavia, had a different fate. Both managed to become independent from Hungary—the former around 1330 and the latter in the 1360s. However, the presence of powerful neighbors often forced these two principalities to accept the status of vassals and to pay tributes, especially to the Turks, who began to expand their influence in that area in the fifteenth century. Yet, there were also some Wallachians and Moldavians who refused this dependence. For example, the Prince of Wallachia, Vlad Țepeș (known as the Impaler) (1456–1462), stopped paying tributes and attacked the Turks south of the Danube. This provoked the reaction of the sultan who deposed him and put on the throne his brother who accepted submission to the Turks.

More successes were obtained by the Prince of Moldavia, Stephen the Great (1457–1504). Thanks to his diplomatic and military skills, he managed to halt the expansionism of his powerful neighbors, i.e. the Hungarians, the Poles, and the Turks. Taking advantage of the rivalry among them, Stephen the Great declared himself vassal of his neighbors, avoiding their sovereignty when the conditions were favorable to him. Moreover he did not fail to face them on the battlefield, obtaining important successes both against the Hungarians and the Turks.

When the latter occupied most of Hungary in 1541, Moldavia and Transylvania were forced to accept the status of autonomous principalities under Turkish sovereignty, thus avoiding military occupation but the sultan often appointed the rulers of these two regions. Profiting from the strong discontent created by the heavy taxation of the Turks, in 1594 the Prince of Wallachia, Michael the Brave, joined the anti-Turkish alliance promoted by the pope. After numerous victories against the Turks, Michael turned his attention to Moldavia and Transylvania, which he occupied in 1599 and 1600 respectively. For the first time since Roman times the area corresponding roughly to modern Romania was once again united. In this way Michael made dangerous and powerful enemies who could not stand the presence of a strong state in an area they wanted to control. The union among the three principalities was short-lived and ended in 1601 with the assassination of Michael by the general of the Habsburg troops who aimed to become the prince of Transylvania. Even though this union lasted only for a brief period, Michael the Brave became a radiant symbol for those who wanted to create a united and powerful Romania in the nineteenth and twentieth centuries.

It is therefore no coincidence that the first film with a medieval and early modern setting of the Ceauşescu era was about Michael the Brave. In 1971, shortly after the Romanian refusal to support the Russian invasion of Czechoslovakia in 1968 and to adhere strictly to the policies of the Soviet Union, *Mihai Viteazul* (*Michael the Brave*, known as *Last Crusade* outside Romania) by Sergiu Nicolaescu was released, recounting the life of that prince of Wallachia.

As in 1600, Romania was again strong in the early 1970s and making itself heard by its powerful neighbors. The film was also addressed to foreigners and was therefore a way to present the history of an important phase of Romania's creation and its successes abroad. The financial investment of the Romanian state in that film was considerable. A deal was struck with Columbia-Warner and the movie was dubbed in English and distributed in forty countries and to eighteen television channels. The Romanian army provided several thousand soldiers who were utilized as extras in the battle scenes.

Not coincidentally, the film begins by emphatically (and inaccurately from a historical point of view) emphasizing that the three principalities that will form modern Romania represented the last obstacle between a divided Europe and the Turks eager to conquer Vienna—a likely allusion to the fact that in the 1970s Romania played a similar role with regard to Russia. The film implicitly presents Wallachia as the engine of Romanian unity, thus providing legitimacy to the modern central power of Romania whose capital, Bucharest, is located in that region. It is also suggested that most of the real Romanians were to be found in Wallachia, which, according to the inhabitants of that area, distinguished itself by the absence of descendants of other ethnic groups like in Moldavia and especially in Transylvania. By presenting a clear division between good and evil, the film legitimizes the right of the Wallachians to reunite the Romanian lands and to rule them.

Michael had not fought for personal interests nor to expand his power, but to build the Romanian motherland and create the identity of the Romanians. After having acquired the title of prince by cheating the Turks, Michael incites his men to revolt, pointing out that they slept for too long and that it was time to wake up and find unity, a concept that is emphasized several times in the movie. Michael highlights that all those speaking his language live in those three principalities and that they have been divided by enemies and it was time to put an end to that situation. To the former prince of Transylvania who talks about 'our nations', Michael replies that there is only one nation, that of his ancestors, namely the land of the Romanians. In the clash against the prince of Moldavia, supported by the Poles, he manages to convince the foot soldiers of the Moldavian army, i.e. members of the Romanian-speaking popular classes, not to fight, calling them brothers. The Poles flee and Michael's soldiers and the Moldavian infantrymen hug each other calling each other brothers. The unity is not only political but above all spiritual. Michael awakens their common identity, reminding his men that their destiny was now fulfilled and those who were born from the same mother and spoke the same language (Wallachians, Transylvanians, and Moldavians) were reunited. There is also a reference to the relevance of the legacy left by the ancient Romans to the people of that area who were proving to be equal to those ancient conquerors who had merged with the Dacians.

The fight for unity was also a fight of the people, not one of the usual wars among nobles. Indeed, the humble are with Michael and ready to face all the sufferings to reach the goal of unity, and the prince of Transylvania appears scandalized that Michael has involved the lower classes in the fight and accuses Michael of having unleashed the mob against the elites. Moreover, Michael highlights the difference between him and his Christian adversaries when he points out that he and his men fight against an army of mercenaries.

Michael is therefore a patriot who succeeds in instilling the sense of belonging to the Romanian motherland also in the other two principalities inhabited by mixed populations. The film also emphasizes that the non-Romanian inhabitants of those principalities were to be looked upon with suspicion because they plotted against that unit. However, the director does not neglect to mention that foreigners were the elites of those two principalities, especially in Transylvania. Both by their behavior and their appearance they are presented as the opposite of Michael and his men. For example some members of the Transylvanian elites look like stereotypical Hungarians with long mustaches. While Michael and his men are engaged in harsh wars against the Turks, the prince of Transylvania and his nobles spend their time in feasts and tournaments. Their clothes are colorful and opulent, while those of the Wallachians are sober and dark. The treacherous behavior of those Transylvanians, always ready to betray their promises, is contrasted by the exemplary behavior and spirit of sacrifice of Michael and his followers. The peoples of Transylvania and Moldavia are, however, on Michael's side. Among them are the true Romanians. They are ready to adhere to Michael's cause, to help him and to bear the sacrifices. Notably, the people of Transylvania welcome Michael in their cities and the colors of the clothes some of them wear bring to mind the flag of modern Romania.

Michael is therefore presented as the opposite of his adversaries. For example, his predecessor is remembered as a sadistic ruler who enjoys punishing those who dare to disobey him by impaling them while he feasts. Michael represents a symbol of self-denial, always ready to sacrifice everything for the good of the country. He always leads his soldiers in battle and does not hesitate to have on his side his young son who dies on the battlefield. The motherland is placed before everything, even personal affection and love. Michael also knows how to act as a diplomat and is ready to repress his pride for the sake of the unity of the country, but never exceeds certain limits. He keeps his dignity intact and does not humiliate himself in front of foreigners. In fact, he accepts to become a vassal of the prince of Transylvania in order to obtain the help of his troops, but he refuses to prostrate himself in front of the sultan to whom he asks to give him the title of prince of Wallachia. He also refuses the offer of the Muslim ruler to remain in Istanbul and become an important and rich general. He rejects a similar offer from the emperor as well and asks the sovereign only to give him the opportunity to rule over his motherland. The fact that in the 1950s Michael was presented by the Romanian historiography as an agent of the Habsburg Empire is therefore completely erased and Michael is included among the builders of the motherland. Michael's death and the end of the unity are not shown, but there is a clear allusion to them at the end of the film. As it happened with Burebista, eliminated by Dacian traitors shortly after having obtained the unity of Dacia, Michael's work was not ephemeral. His example would in fact provide a model for the future.

A second film depicting Romanian medieval history was released in 1974 to celebrate the five hundredth anniversary of the victory of the Moldavians against the Turks at the Battle of Vaslui: *Ştefan cel Mare-Vaslui 1475* (*Stephen the Great-Vaslui 1475*) by Mircea Drăgan. The movie focuses on the deeds of the Prince of Moldavia, Stephen III (1457–1504), who led his men to victory. As in the other Romanian films, *Stephen the Great* also emphasizes the theme of the great man necessary for the construction of Romania and the Romanians. The reference to Ceauşescu, the great man of modern Romania, is obvious. It is no coincidence that the film begins with a quotation from Ceauşescu's speech about the statue of Stephen placed in Vaslui where modern Romanians were reminded of the role played by the Moldavians in the defense of their homeland. Without a ruler like Stephen III, the history of Moldavia would have been a complete disaster. It is noteworthy that, like Michael the Brave, Stephen the Great is also loved by the people.

In this film, the most relevant message is the need to defend the motherland at all costs from external enemies who threaten to conquer it. The movie promotes the idea of self-sacrifice over liberation. It is necessary to fight even if this will cause death and destruction. In this case, too, parallels with the modern era were evident. Within the portrayal of the fifteenth century Turks, there were clear references to the Russians of the 1970s. Also clear at that time was the challenge to Russia in the exalting of the most famous ruler of Moldavia, which in the fifteenth century was about twice the size of modern Moldavia. Due to its support of Nazi Germany, Romania lost a part of those territories after World War II and that area became a republic of the Soviet Union under the name of Moldova.

The same themes of the great man, the necessity of defending the motherland from the external enemy, and the necessity of sacrifice appear also in another film, *Vlad Ţepeş* (*Vlad the Impaler*, 1978) by Doru Năstase. The need to redefine the figure of the prince, who inspired the creation of the fictional character of Dracula abroad, as well as the more and more authoritarian regime of Ceauşescu, led to emphasize the fact that the drastic punishments enacted by Prince Vlad were necessary in order to restore the internal order and to frighten the enemies (such ideas were already widespread in Romania since the nineteenth century). According to the movie, Vlad is a good prince who thinks about defending his people and does not sentence anyone to death unjustly. He also meets with the Moldavian prince Stephen III and the two rulers agree that it is better not to fight each other but to face their common enemies: the Turks in the south, the Hungarians in the northwest, and the Poles in the north-east.

Vlad acts for national defense and the creation of a motherland that is surrounded by enemies. This is the rhetoric of the besieged fortress which was strongly emphasized in the 1970s by the Romanian government, simultaneously pointing out the need to apply harsh laws to all those who transgress in order to protect the homeland and its people. In the movie, Romania's internal adversaries are found among the German-speaking peoples of Transylvania and the nobility of Wallachia, who are always ready to plot. They are also credited with creating the black legend of Prince Vlad as a bloodthirsty monster. As with Michael the Brave, there is an invitation to give due consideration to the legacy of Vlad. At one point, the prince of Wallachia ponders on his actions and says that he did not build churches, monasteries, and citadels, but he built in the soul of the nation and cleaned up it. Therefore, Vlad too, had the right to be considered as one of the founding fathers of modern Romania.

Despite the exemplarity of Stephen the Great and Vlad displayed in the movies, their depiction was probably too close to Ceaușescu and therefore Romanian spectators preferred the theme of unity in the film on Michael the Brave (also characterized by better acting and directing) to the point that *Michael the Brave* became one of the most ever watched Romanian movies.

Inspiring independence

Heralded by a strong publicity campaign and bitter controversy in both Scotland and England, *Braveheart* was released in 1995 by Australian director and actor Mel Gibson, who also played the lead role in the film and co-produced it. *Braveheart* tells the story of William Wallace, a Scottish warrior who led a revolt against the English at the end of the thirteenth century. The film presents a very clear division between the good guys (the Scottish commoners who sided with Wallace) and the bad guys (the English and the Scottish nobles). It also clearly underlines that Wallace's use of violence against the English was legitimate and sacrosanct—the hero, portrayed as a peaceful man of house and family, had been forced to act after the oppressors nefariously killed his young wife. The episode constitutes an awakening for the hero, and Wallace's individual revenge is transformed into a righteous collective vindication, the struggle of the Scots to gain their freedom from the English oppressors.

The plot of the film is loosely based on a fifteenth-century epic poem, Blind Harry's *The Acts and Deeds of Sir William Wallace, Knight of Elderslie*, a text unanimously acknowledged to be unreliable for reconstructing William Wallace's history. In defense of his work, the American screenwriter Randall Wallace said: 'Is Blind Harry true? I don't know. I know that it spoke to my heart and that's what matters to me, that it spoke to my heart.' These statements speak for themselves and require no comment. It is the classic patch that is worse than the hole it intends to repair. However, it must be admitted that the screenwriter and perhaps the director did not always demonstrate such a disregard for reliability of the sources. The pair tried to counter the expected harsh criticism by including the following statement at the beginning of the film.

> I shall tell you of William Wallace. Historians from England will say I am a liar, but history is written by those who have hanged heroes.

This is undoubtedly a very clever stunt that would seem to stifle any criticism the film's detractors could have given. Indeed, history is often written by the victors. However, it should be noted that, at least among serious professional historians, it is a commonly accepted practice not to take for granted the information contained in sources, especially narrative and biased ones. Rather than aiming to reconstruct the truth, professional historians examine the opinions and ideas that texts express.

This clever opening statement prevents the historian from examining *Braveheart* by using the same methodology utilized for the other films analyzed in this book. From the historian's point of view, however, it should be noted that the clever move stops there. In fact, the rest of the film is marked by absurd assertions and chronological errors. Suffice it to say that those two sentences are followed by a brief historical introduction that highlights serious linguistic and historical problems. The English king is defined as a pagan, a surprising statement considering that English sovereigns had always been Christian since the seventh century. The screenwriter and the director obviously wanted to emphasize the cruelty of that ruler, but pagan has an entirely different meaning. In addition to numerous anachronisms such as anticipating the use of kilts and bagpipes by several centuries, *Braveheart* contains ridiculous chronological errors. The worst one concerns the reference to the love story between the hero and the wife of the heir to the English throne, the future Edward II. In the film, Princess Isabella, who was French, reveals to the near-to-death King Edward I that she was pregnant with Wallace's child who would destroy Edward II. In reality, Isabella was three years old at the time, living in France, and married Edward's son when Edward II was already king. Twenty years after Wallace's death, Isabella, with the help of her son and her lover, deposed Edward II and then had him killed.

Unlike the other films examined in this book which express problems and demands well rooted in the years in which they were made, *Braveheart* is a remarkable example of a film that does not invent certain claims but rather, through the simple messages it conveys about what is right and wrong, manages to popularize those claims and, above all, to make them seem justified. It is crucial to note that this happened because the film was made and viewed in a very specific historical context. In all likelihood, if it had been released fifteen years earlier, these aspects would not have emerged, and it would only have been seen as a compelling epic film.

With the end of the Soviet Union in 1991, the need for a strong and united western bloc to counter the Communist one ended as well. At the beginning of the 1990s, several areas (the so-called small homelands) claimed independence from the central authorities, who, according to their supporters, were the direct heirs of the powers that in the past had subjugated and exploited those small homelands; such claims arose in conjunction with the attempts to expand and strengthen the European Union. I doubt that the screenwriter and the director were aware of these feelings. Nevertheless, the spectacularity of the film and its compelling story, in addition to the fact that it amplified and legitimized independence from such authorities led to the success of the film in Scotland and Europe. It is no coincidence that the Scottish independence movement, which until that moment had not received much support, began its great rise.

For the same reasons, that film was very popular in other European 'small homelands', especially in those areas where there were political movements that, in the name of a pseudo-Celtic brotherhood, believed to have intimate affinities with Scotland and to share the oppression suffered by foreign powers. For example, in Italy, the end of the Soviet Union gave way to a profound political crisis that led to the disappearance of the largest conservative political party and a considerable downsizing and fractioning of the main left-wing party. Not coincidentally, in those years, the Northern League, a party that aimed to obtain the independence (or at least a strong autonomy) of northern Italy from the Italian state arose. The leaders of that party tried to create a historical basis for their claims, pointing out that there had always existed a people of northern Italy of Celtic origin who had suffered the oppression of foreign peoples. A great fan of *Braveheart* (awarded in February 1996 with several Oscar awards), the leader of the Northern League, Umberto Bossi, claiming to have been inspired by William Wallace, attacked the central power during the speeches for the political elections of April 1996, pointing out that for thousands of years 'Rome the Thief' had oppressed and exploited the Italians of the North as the English had done with the Scots. Center-left newspapers ironically nicknamed the politician 'MacBossi' and depicted him in cartoons wearing the Scottish kilt. But that ironic tone soon ceased in light of the election results of that year which saw the victory of the center-right coalition, with which the Northern League had sided, and which confirmed the remarkable growth of that party (in some areas of the North it received the majority of votes).

The United States experienced a different reaction. After twelve years of Republican presidents, a Democrat had been elected, sparking a revival of movements from nostalgic Southern Confederates and white supremacists who were traditionally opposed to a strong central authority and critical of the liberal values typical of the Northeastern part of the United States. *Braveheart* was praised because 'it appeals to all the things that New York despises, namely Christian devotion, populism, patriotism, home rule, self defense, well-defined sex roles, traditional morality and self sacrifice for a noble cause.'

More proof that there are no simple recipes for making a successful film and that *Braveheart* fits into a well-defined historical context of which the screenwriter and director were unaware lies in the failed success of the 2000 film *The Patriot*. The movie also stars Mel Gibson and uses a similar narrative structure as that of *Braveheart* (the villains are always the English and the hero takes up arms following the evil deeds they have done), transporting this oppression to the years of the American War of Independence. This film did not spark any independence movements.

So much noise for so little. A *Braveheart* in Italian Sauce

The leaders of the Northern League hoped to match the success of *Braveheart* with their own film, *Barbarossa* (2009), directed by the Italian filmmaker Renzo Martinelli and co-financed with public funding. When the movie was released, the Northern League was part of the coalition of parties that governed Italy, but strong pressure to obtain funding from public television had already been exerted during the period when that coalition was not in power. For example, in December 2007, in a phone call between the leader of the largest party of that alliance, Silvio Berlusconi, and an Italian public television executive, the Italian politician asked for public funds to produce that film, pointing out that the leader of the Northern League cared a great deal about it (the phone call was intercepted and made public by a well-known Italian weekly).

Barbarossa was part of the Northern League's project to provide historical roots for its independence demands that would appeal to emotion, strengthen the sense of unity and identity, and gather the consent of the largest possible number of inhabitants of northern Italy. This went hand in hand with the assumption that, both in the past and in the contemporary world, the inhabitants of northern Italy had been subjected to fiscal, political, and ethnic oppression by non-native powers. Among those roots was the 'Societas Lombardie' (Society of Lombardy)—referred to by modern historians as the Lombard League—an alliance created in 1167 by a number of northern Italian cities to oppose the German Emperor Frederick Barbarossa, who had re-established imperial authority over northern Italy. Taking that event as the emblem of the northern Italians' struggle against an oppressive foreign power, the Northern League took its name from that alliance and, among its symbols, chose a medieval warrior with a sword pointing upwards. According to the leaders of that party, the latter represented Albert of Giussano, who was believed to have been the promoter of the Lombard League (the first source that mentions him is from the fourteenth century). Each year the leaders of the Northern League celebrate a festival on the day of the year and in the place, Pontida, where the oath that had sealed that coalition would have taken place (the first to mention Pontida is a sixteenth-century author).

Despite his title, the main character of *Barbarossa* is Albert of Giussano, a Milanese blacksmith who takes up arms to defend his city from the German sovereign. In the clash, which ended with the fall of Milan, Albert's two brothers die. To avenge their death and the destruction of his city, the hero of the film creates a chosen body of warriors, the Company of Death, with whom he leads many cities of Northern Italy, united in the Lombard League in Pontida, in the fight against the German sovereign. He is also the architect of the Lombard League's victory over Barbarossa at Legnano.

The film plays upon the theme of the freedom of the people of Northern Italy on several occasions. Unlike *Braveheart*, however, *Barbarossa* does not present a clear division between good guys and bad guys. In fact, the German emperor and his men are not portrayed as the incarnation of evil, and their image is therefore very far from the one created in Mel Gibson's film for the English. Martinelli has stated that he wanted to show that even Barbarossa had had a human side. Ironically, a similar operation had already been carried out by historians of northern Italy in the sixteenth and eighteenth centuries to highlight their loyalty as subjects of the Empire. In turn, the Milanese are not always depicted as innocent victims like William Wallace's companions. For example, Barbarossa refuses the invitation of one of his generals to intervene militarily and to punish the Milanese aggressions against the Lombard city of Lodi. He prefers instead to use diplomacy and only to use force when the Milanese arrogantly refuse to resolve the conflicts peacefully.

Contrary to *Braveheart*, Martinelli's film also lacks a setting, symbols, and physiognomies with which viewers in northern Italy could identify. In order to keep costs down, *Barbarossa* was largely shot in Romania with Romanian extras, i.e., people whose emigration to Italy was vehemently opposed by members of the Northern League. The role of the hero was entrusted to an Israeli model and actor, Raz Degan, well known in Italy (especially among female audience), who undoubtedly gives the film a touch of glamour, but whose physiognomy most likely did not correspond to the northern canons present in the minds of the Northern League supporters. The director uses characters that probably never existed, such as Albert of Giussano, mentions the anachronistic concept of the unity of northern Italy, insists on the struggle for freedom of the people of that area, and includes the leader of the modern Northern League (in reality unrecognizable) among those swearing the oath in Pontida. At the same time, however, he correctly mentions some characteristics of those events: the aggressive policy of the Milanese against other cities in northern Italy and the support of the latter for Barbarossa. It almost seems that the director did not fully understand what his clients wanted. These peculiarities, combined with Martinelli's obvious limitations (*Barbarossa* is far from the dynamism and pathos of *Braveheart*, is very boring, and is so unimaginative as to copy various scenes from famous films), meant that *Barbarossa*, in addition to being massacred by the reviewers of all newspapers for the flaws in style and content (the only exception was the newspaper of the Northern League) and harshly criticized by some professional medievalists, was a big failure at the box office and was appreciated only by the Northern League supporters who resided in the symbolic places of their party, such as Legnano and Pontida.

The leaders of the Northern league's attempts to create a historical tradition and an ethnic identity for political and independence purposes—characterized by a lack of discernment—was outdated and could only be successful among poorly educated people who constituted the hard core of that party. In fact, that project was based on inventions of traditions made in the nineteenth century in a different context and with completely different purposes. Suffice to say that in that period the goal was to create an Italian state that would include the areas that were part of the Habsburg Empire (Lombardy and the North East of the Peninsula) and the small states in which Italy was divided. When *Barbarossa* was released, the consensus for the Northern League had already reached all those in northern Italy who were willing to accept the demands of that party. Soon, the party began to lose votes, a factor that led the new leaders to put aside its northern and independentist vocation and historical inventions and to transform the Northern League into a traditional right-wing party. Since then, it has achieved a success of votes at the national level unthinkable for the Northern League.

3

LEFTIST SOCIAL AND POLITICAL TOPICS IN 1960S AND 1970S MOVIES

In the United States and Western Europe during the 1960s and 1970s the lengthy process of national schooling and the significant increase in the numbers of university students helped to raise awareness among a large number of young people about social and political issues, thus providing the ideal conditions to create a movement of young persons who, not limiting themselves to the traditional clash between generations, spread a youth counterculture that manifested itself in a strong desire to criticize the world created by their parents. This movement and counterculture did not have clear-cut characteristics, yet themes such as the rights of the oppressed and women, the condemnation both of the most blatant forms of exploitation of the working class and of the environment implemented by the capitalist system, and the criticism of the family's traditional structure were very common in those years. To these was added pacifism, an ideal that went hand in hand with protests against the war in Vietnam, whose horrors and violence against the civilian population could be witnessed in Europe and the United States thanks to extensive television coverage and photojournalism of that conflict. This atmosphere of contestation and renewal also involved the intellectual world. Although this was not a complete novelty, in that period women, the subordinate classes, the marginalized, and in general all the oppressed became more and more the object of academic research and the arts.

Saint Francis, 1960s-counterculture style

A film about a character from the Middle Ages that was greatly influenced by the turmoil that animated many young people in the 1960s is undoubtedly *Brother Sun, Sister Moon* (1972) by Italian director Franco Zeffirelli. It narrates the first part of the life of one of the most famous saints of the Catholic Church and patron saint of

DOI: 10.4324/9781003153139-4

Italy, Francis of Assisi (d. 1226), i.e. from his spiritual transformation to the pope's approval of the conduct of life adopted by him and his companions. Since Zeffirelli invented numerous episodes and changed various historical details, it is necessary to summarize what the first Francis's biographies, composed by friars who had personally known him, report: the *First Life* by Thomas of Celano and the *Legend of the Three Companions*.

Francis was the son of Peter of Bernardone, a cloth merchant, and Pica, and was born in Assisi (central Italy) around 1181/1182. Although he was educated to be a merchant like his father, at whose store he worked, he displayed a penchant for the mentality and lifestyle of the nobles by spending the money he earned and borrowed on expensive clothes, gifts, entertainment, and banquets with his friends. In 1203, while in his early 20s, Francis participated in the war between Assisi and Perugia, was captured, and spent a year in prison where he fell ill. After returning home, he succeeded in recovering physically, but was affected by a strong personal crisis; he lost his self-esteem and interest for all that had attracted him previously.

After a few years he tried to return to his old aspirations and join the troop of a fellow citizen about to leave for a campaign in southern Italy in the hope of being knighted. He spent a great deal of money on clothes and weapons to equip himself (which he eventually gave to a poor knight) and set off on his new adventure. After a few miles Francis began to feel very tired and therefore decided to stop and rest. In his sleep he heard the voice of God inviting him to return to Assisi where he would be told what he had to do. He went back home and resumed his previous lifestyle, having parties and banquets with friends and spending lavishly. He kept working in his father's store and decided to spend more time at home and began to give more alms and bread to the indigent. To poor priests he donated the objects that their churches lacked. During this phase, at the suggestion of the bishop of Assisi, Francis often retired to a cave to pray and meditate. There the devil persecuted him by making him appear 'a hunchbacked and deformed woman of Assisi' and telling him that he would become like her if he kept going to that place. He went on a pilgrimage to Rome, continued to give gifts to the poor, and tried to live like them for a few hours by exchanging his clothes for those of a poor man and asking for charity on the steps of St. Peter's Basilica. During one of his horseback rides outside Assisi he met a leper to whom he gave some money, kissed and hugged him. A few days later he repeated these gestures in a leper colony.

Not feeling ready to change his life radically, he continued to live as usual until, when in the church of St. Damiano, he heard Christ say to him: 'Francis, can't you see that my house is falling down? Go and repair it.' He left the church happy, because now he knew what he had to do. He went to a nearby town, sold all his goods and his horse, and then handed over the proceeds to the priest of St. Damiano. The latter, however, refused the money for fear of the reaction of the family of Francis, who then threw the coins on the windowsill of a church (see primary source A). In order not to be caught by his angry father for that gesture, Francis hid and spent a period of uncertainty oscillating between moments of despair and moments of joy.

One day, feeling confident of his choice, he left his hiding place and went home. Because of his appearance—he was pale and thin for fasting and dressed in rags—the inhabitants of Assisi took him for a fool and began to make fun of him and some children threw stones and mud at him. Upon hearing this, his father took Francis, beat him, and locked him in a room of his house. During Peter's absence, his wife freed her son. The father became even more angry and decided to denounce his son to the secular authorities of Assisi, who asked the young man to report to them. Francis refused to obey, declaring that he was now a penitent and was therefore under the jurisdiction of the Church. Peter then turned to the bishop who summoned Francis and told him that the Church could not accept money that did not belong to him. The young man then took off all his clothes and gave them to his father together with the money he still had and said that from that moment on his only father would be God. He then went to live in a leper colony and began to restore some churches among which was that of St. Damiano.

His first companion was a wealthy fellow citizen named Bernard who, after inviting Francis to his home and talking with him for almost a whole night, decided to give all his goods to the poor and to join him. Soon others followed his example. Having reached the symbolic number of twelve, they decided to go to Rome to obtain official recognition of their activities. Thanks to the bishop of Assisi, they met Cardinal John Colonna, who, after unsuccessfully trying to convince Francis to accept a traditional monastic rule, decided to present him to Pope Innocent III.

As proof that the meeting was not immediately as idyllic as Francis's biographers narrate, there is the testimony of an English author of the thirteenth century, according to whom the pontiff told Francis to return to the pigsty from which he had come. Innocent III and several cardinals considered his desire to follow the evangelical precepts strange and too difficult to put into practice. However, impressed by Francis's perseverance and devotion, the pope finally approved his rule (see primary sources B and C).

Inspired by the conduct of life of her fellow citizen, a young woman of Assisi named Clare decided to imitate him by leaving her family and assuming the leadership of a group of women eager to live according to the teachings of Jesus. Francis's biographers do not mention anything else about her. In the biography of Clare it is reported that she wanted to meet her fellow citizen when he had already become famous for his exemplary conduct of life. After some meetings that took place secretly in order not to arouse gossip, the young woman, at the suggestion of Francis, decided to devote herself to religious life. She went therefore to Francis and his companions who cut her hair and, after having assumed the signs of the penitent and having spent some days in two churches of Assisi, on the advice of Francis, she settled down in St. Damiano, where she spent her life in seclusion (see primary source D).

In the case of *Brother Sun, Sister Moon*, rather than influences exerted by the present on the plot of the film, it is more correct to speak of the invention of a well-structured series of episodes aimed at establishing an explicit link between the experiences and ideals of Francis and his companions and those of many young people of the 1960s. The director thus addressed the latter and those who sympathized with their ideas by saying that Francis was one of them.

In fact, the movie shows a Francis who was against the exploitation of the working class. His visit to his father's workshop upsets him and causes him intense pain for the conditions of the workers. Not only is that place in a basement with very little light and air, but the employees carry out extremely tiring activities that are clearly harmful to their health. There are also persons of both sexes and all ages among them, and there is even a woman with a small child and an elderly man who can barely move.

To give more strength to this message the director used knowledge and mental patterns characteristic of many young people of the 1960s. Indeed, those scenes seem to have been inspired by an episode of the Buddha's life made known to many young people of those years through the book *Siddhartha* by Herman Hesse, originally published in 1922 but particularly popular in the 1960s and in the 1970s. Before becoming Buddha, Siddhartha was an Indian prince whose father prevented him from leaving his palace where the young man had only known pleasures and had always been in contact with young, healthy, and beautiful people. One day he managed to get out of his gilded prison and seeing a poor man, an old man, and a dead man, was exposed to the harshness of real life. Deeply affected by that experience, he decided to renounce all his privileges and embark on the quest to achieve his own spiritual perfection. As it happened for Siddhartha, also for the Francis of the film that experience is an important stage for his transformation. Zeffirelli's Francis, however, is a character of the Western world and was created in a period in which, in addition to the search for spiritual perfection, there was a desire among young people to perform actions that would improve the world. Unlike that prestigious model, the Francis of *Brother Sun, Sister Moon* is not limited to individual transformation, but alleviates the suffering of his father's employees by no longer making them work for a day and taking them out into the sun. It seems obvious that it was a long time since they were able to do that. Particularly touching is the scene of the joy felt by the already mentioned elderly worker whom Francis holds up as he leaves the basement.

The Francis of the film does not fail to exhibit his rejection of the material goods that his father cares so much about. His first gesture is only a brief but significant nod that indicates his realization of the falsity of values and above all the abject basis of the well-being in which he has lived up to that moment. While his father shows him with great satisfaction the riches acquired thanks to the misfortunes caused to many people by the war (Peter emphasizes his joy for what he has achieved saying with laughter: 'and there are people who speak ill of the war'), Francis takes a coin and slowly looks at it as if it were dung.

Also relevant is how the director shows Francis's rejection and sharing of his father's possessions with others. The unspectacular episode narrated in Thomas of Celano's biography, which states that the young man offered the money obtained from the sale of some fabrics to a priest to finance the reconstruction of a church in ruins and, after the latter refuses to accept it, threw it on the window sill of a church, in the film is transformed into a blatant gesture and a scene with a strong visual impact in line with the ideals of the 1960s. In fact, the young man gives his parent's precious fabrics to passers-by by throwing them from a window of the merchant's house, a very high tower. The choice of that place is not only due to the need to make that action more spectacular. It takes place in the most evident sign of the father's wealth, that is the house with two towers, medieval equivalents of skyscrapers, the seats of modern economic power. In this regard, it should be remembered that it is impossible that a merchant like Francis's father could own a tower (only the richest noble families could afford this).

In order to emphasize the difference in values between the father and the son and the harsh reaction of Peter to his son's behavior, Zeffirelli distorts the biography of the saint even in the later scenes that show the final separation of Francis from his father. Peter, at the sight of what his son is doing with his possessions, becomes furious, beats Francis, and asks first the secular authorities and then the bishop of Assisi to intervene against the ungrateful son who always had everything he wanted from him and repaid him by giving away the fruit of a lifetime's work.

The film does not fail to mention the theme of feminism giving considerable importance to the character of Clare. First of all, she is portrayed as a sort of spiritual guide for Francis, who, besides being present and giving a sign of approval at every stage of the young man's spiritual change, encourages him on that difficult path. Clare has such a role even before Francis's spiritual travails. To the young man who spent a night of revelry before leaving for war and is probably chasing her to indulge in further pleasure, Clare shows that there is more to the world than entertainment and that there are those who suffer and need help. The young woman in fact went out early to bring bread to some lepers. Clare also witnesses Francis's return to Assisi after he probably fled the battlefield, the initial point of his transformation.

After having recovered physically, the young man seems uncertain and confused about what to do, but she reassures him by saying:

> Everyone thinks you are crazy, you know that. When you went to war, people said you were good and smart and now they say you are crazy because you make bird noises, run after butterflies, and look at flowers. In my opinion you were crazy before, not now.

Clare smiles in a sign of approval when, during the mass, Francis expresses his refusal for that ritual devoid of spiritual meaning and when he decides to abandon everything connected to his previous life, clothes included.

FIGURE 3.1   Clare tells Francis what is right and what is wrong (screenshot from *Brother Sun, Sister Moon*)

Emblematic is the phrase that Clare says to Francis when she tells him that she wishes to follow the evangelical precepts together with him and his companions.

> I do not want to be loved, but I want to love. I do not want to be understood, but I want to understand.

These two simple sentences in which the passive form of the verb is rejected while the active form is appreciated, indicate that, like her peers of the 1960s, Clare desired to be an active not a passive element in the society of her time. Unlike the Clare of the Middle Ages who, having received the approval of Francis, followed the rules of the medieval Church by creating a female community distinctly separate from Francis's companions, the Clare of *Brother Sun, Sister Moon* joins Francis's group that closely resembles a hippie community. In harmony with the spirit of this type of community, but completely anachronistic for the Middle Ages, is the message of the song that accompanies the celebration of the restoration of the church of St. Damiano by Francis and his companions. It is in fact an invitation not to get caught up in the frenetic pace of a life marked by false material values.

In line with the aspirations of many young people of the 1960s who wanted to find inner peace in nature and to have respect for the environment are the scenes in which Francis, having recovered physically, begins his transformation by immersing himself in nature (the point in which Clare tells Francis that in her opinion he was crazy before and that now he behaved well takes place in the context of an idyllic landscape). These scenes are not anachronistic but present a Francis with attitudes exactly opposite to those described in his first biography, where it is reported that in that phase the young man discovered that the sight of fields and vineyards did not give him any joy as before and he considered foolish those who were attached to such things.

There is no lack of reference to the exaggerated use of violence by the authorities against young people who peacefully protested against the injustices of the Western world. The police and the army sometimes intervened so violently as to cause even the death of some demonstrators (the bloodiest episode occurred at the US university Kent State on May 4, 1970). In the film the bishop of Assisi orders some soldiers to close the church of St. Damiano, and they kill a person opposed to that action. In this case the director does not limit himself to inventing an episode that never happened, but rather turns the historical reality upside down. The bishop of Assisi, in fact, was one of the main supporters of Francis's conduct of life.

The fact that such a perfect exemplar of evangelical life like Francis had fought before his transformation did not fit well with the image of Francis that Zeffirelli wanted to project. In order to show that the saint of Assisi rejected violence even before his transformation, the film alludes to the fact that Francis left the battlefield; neither the fight nor the flight are shown, but the young man's horse is seen wandering alone after the battle (in the English version of the movie we hear the voice of his friend Bernard calling him without getting any response). The next scene showing Francis returning to Assisi alone completely distraught and his father telling those watching that his son was not a coward and returned because he was ill further reinforces the impression that Francis left the battlefield.

On the other hand, the aforementioned Bernard is presented as a Vietnam volunteer who is disillusioned and disgusted with what he did during war and who, upon returning home, is unable to adjust to the normalcy of his former life and communicate what happened to him to those who had not participated in that war; he wants to find a true ideal to follow and put into practice. Having returned to Assisi after taking part in a crusade (a military endeavor, which, like the Vietnam War, seemed to many young people to be for an ideal but which turned out to be a conflict for material interests), Bernard is celebrated as a hero but he is not proud about it at all and remarks that 'crusades are not things to celebrate.' To a friend who pretends not to have heard that statement and asks him how many Muslims he killed, Bernard replies bitterly, 'too many.' He explicitly reveals to Francis his disappointment with his actions in the Holy Land, feelings felt by many young volunteers who went to Vietnam.

> When I fought in the Crusades I understood what it means to feel deceived in one's ideals, to become ourselves champions of lies and injustice in the

name of Christ. Since I understood these things, I lost the happiness of living. Now I would give everything I have to be able to find it again.

The film also hints at the suspicion and sometimes hostility that the youth of the movement aroused among some members of the working classes, who doubted that children of the wealthy classes could be useful to their causes. In fact, Francis and his companions are harvesting wheat together with some peasants and at lunch they hope to receive bread from them. When one of the laborers is about to hand it over because they have worked and are poorer than they are, the head of the reapers objects stating that they are not poor, but 'sons of the masters, sons of the rich', and if the peasants give them bread there would be less food for them. Francis then replies 'we are all poor', thus underlining that there was no difference between him and those peasants (an allusion to the fact that the young idealists of the 1960s wanted to let the workers know that they sided with them).

Finally, there is a reference to a question that characterized those who wanted to change society, not just to protest or reject the world built by their parents. What was the best strategy to heal society's ills: working within it or outside it? On the occasion of the meeting between the pope and Francis, who went to Rome to ask for approval of his conduct of life, the elderly pontiff makes a statement that highlights the fact that it is impossible to make changes by working within the system because this leads to forgetting ideals and prevents the implementation of reforms.

You have given me dear children great joy and a little nostalgia. At the beginning of my vocation, oh so many years ago, I too began as you did, but in time all that enthusiasm waned. The responsibility of the Church and government got the better of us, as you well see. . . . We are encrusted with wealth and power. You, with your poverty, with your simplicity, were able to humble us.

It is no coincidence that the old man, who has now become a former reformer, and the young man manage to communicate only when the pope takes off his rich cloak and places himself on the same level as Francis, whom he honors by kissing his feet (image 3.2). This is, however, a brief moment of contact because the cardinals, i.e. the system, take possession of the elderly man shortly afterwards, making him wear his rich clothes again, that is to say, making him go back inside the system and cancelling in this way any ambition of reform. It is noteworthy that the film also shows that for those who are perfectly integrated into the system and have never been reformers, not even in their youth, it is inconceivable that anyone of them would attempt to be genuinely in tune, even if only for a brief moment, with the young reformers. To colleagues upset about how the pope behaved with Francis, a cardinal observes that the pope knew what he was doing. His was merely a move to bring the poor back to the Church.

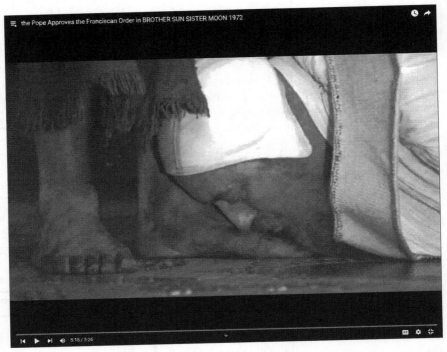

the Pope Approves the Franciscan Order in BROTHER SUN SISTER MOON 1972

5:18 / 5:26

FIGURE 3.2 The pope kisses the feet of Francis (screenshot from *Brother Sun, Sister Moon*)

A Robin Hood disgusted by an unnecessary war

Of all the films based on Robin Hood the one that undoubtedly deviates significantly from the traditional plot is Richard Lester's *Robin and Marian* (1976). The legendary thief who stole from the rich to give to the poor is in fact portrayed as a prematurely aged middle-aged man who dies at the end of the film. In the context of this book, some of the scenes in the film are relevant because Robin is portrayed as a veteran so disgusted with a pointless war that he openly challenges his leader (King Richard), refusing to obey his orders. It is noteworthy that the director does not limit himself only to making allusions to this, but indulges in the event that brought out such feelings.

In the film, in fact, we see Richard besieging a castle situated in his French domains and inhabited only by children, women, and a man, mad and half-blind. The king's objective is to seize a golden statue that he believes is in the castle. Upon learning that the precious object does not actually exist, the king orders Robin and his warriors to attack anyway. The senseless order provokes Robin's reaction and he says to the sovereign.

> I've followed you for twenty years. I fought for you in the Crusade. I've fought for you in France. Show me a soldier and I'll fight him for you now. But I won't slaughter children for a piece of gold that never was.

At yet another refusal to obey his orders, the king has Robin arrested and leads the assault on the castle himself, which ends with the killing of all its occupants.

This part of the film, which portrays leadership that is now devoid of sense, that imposes to fight a ruthless war for a very material purpose, which moreover does not exist, the violence on civilians, including women and children, and the disgust and rejection for a senseless war must be seen in the context of the Vietnam War (officially ended the year before the film was released), not coincidentally marked by those very characteristics. The most terrible example occurred in March 1968, in the village of May Lai, where during the attempt to repel the powerful offensive unleashed in January of that year by the North Vietnamese and their supporters, American soldiers killed more than three hundred civilians (mostly elderly, women and children) because that village had hosted Vietnamese guerrillas.

However, that tragedy was too fresh to be digested and understood by the majority of the American public, who expected amusement and entertainment from a film about Robin Hood. It is therefore no surprise that *Robin and Marian* was a disaster at the box office.

A militant *Song of Roland*

Another 1970s film that greatly distorts its medieval source is *La Chanson de Roland* (*The Song of Roland*, 1978) by French director Frank Cassenti. Probably based on texts transmitted orally and put into writing around 1100, *The Song of Roland* is the first French literary text to have been composed in vernacular, is considered a monument of French literature and civilization, and is therefore believed to be an essential cornerstone of the modern French school system. The medieval poem is a work of fiction, extolling some of the values of the world of nobles and knights, but the plot is a rehash of a real event: the campaign of the Frankish ruler Charlemagne (c. 740–814) against the Muslims in Spain. The expedition, which took place in 778, ended in a deadlock because, after unsuccessfully trying to take Zaragoza, a revolt in Germany forced Charlemagne to return to his dominions. During the crossing of the Pyrenees, the Christian population of the Basques annihilated the rearguard of the Frankish army, commanded by the prefect of Brittany, Roland.

In the poem Charlemagne sends an ambassador, Gano, to the Muslim ruler Marsilius. Devoid of any ethics and envious of Roland, nephew of the Frankish sovereign, Gano plays a double game and organizes with the Muslims an ambush against the rearguard of the Frankish army led, on Gano's advice, by Roland. A huge number of Muslims attacked the troops of Charlemagne's nephew who decided to face the enemies with his few men because to call in help from the rest of the army would have been a dishonor for him. In the course of the fighting Roland kills a large number of Muslims, including their king. Only shortly before his death he blows his horn, thus calling Charlemagne, after which he asks God for forgiveness for his sins and then dies. The archangels Gabriel and

Michael take his soul to heaven. Charlemagne avenges Roland by defeating the Muslims at Zaragoza and condemning Gano to death.

Like the poem, the movie deviates considerably from its source and it was the director himself who explained in interviews the meaning of his version of *The Song of Roland*. Born in Morocco to a French Jewish family and moved as an adolescent to Algeria, then a French colony and theater between the 1950s and the early 1960s of the bloodiest war of independence from a colonial power in the twentieth century, Cassenti first of all did not hide his contempt for that literary text considered to be a cornerstone of Frenchness.

> The epic of Roland and Charlemagne marked my schooling in Algeria, where, in the context of the war, I perceived the racism of that text. It was hard not to make a comparison between Roland's wars, his imperialistic aims, and colonial warfare.

Cassenti also declared that *The Song of Roland* was one of the first ideological texts of the Middle Ages that, in addition to justifying war of conquest and imperialism, aimed to spread the ideas of the nobility and the clergy, and he defined the character of Roland as Fascist.

The director legitimized the changes made in the film by stating that *The Song of Roland* had distorted a historical event for propaganda purposes, an operation similar to that carried out in Hollywood, whose films replaced real history. This reference, however, should not lead one to think that Cassenti wished to correct the distortions of historical reality made in *The Song of Roland* by reconstructing what had really happened. He declared that the Middle Ages interested him because they laid the foundations of modern society. According to him, at that time there was the end of slavery, the beginning of capitalism, the creation of state institutions, and the delineation of social classes and the relationships among them. The first revolts of the oppressed and the first strikes of the working classes occurred in that period as well.

Not surprisingly, Cassenti added that he had been attracted to a story of a fundamental historical period such as the Middle Ages because the temporal distance allowed him to provide a key to understanding the contemporary world. His objective was therefore to highlight the racist and imperialistic features of that fundamental French text, reminding that those characteristics were still present in contemporary France and at the same time suggesting remedies for those evils. His was not only an invitation to reflect on the recent bloody experience of the decolonization of Algeria, but also to what was still happening in France. In fact, the feelings of many French people towards Muslim immigrants from North Africa were extremely negative, feelings that were exacerbated by the serious economic crisis of the 1970s and which led to a law in 1974 that restricted immigration from France's former colonies.

The film describes the journey of some thirteenth-century pilgrims to Santiago of Compostela in Spain. They are joined by some actors and a jester who each evening tells his fellow travelers about *The Song of Roland* that the actors enact. Cassenti's provocative messages appear right from the actor chosen to play the role of the main character, assigned to German actor Klaus Kinski who, thanks to the hard features of his face and his expression, was famous for having played the role of the villain in several movies. Both the face and the actions of Cassenti's Roland are evil. At the beginning of the film we see Roland—the only Frankish warrior wearing a helmet with horns worthy of the worst Viking parody (image 3.3)—who, in front of an impassive Charlemagne, orders an archer to kill one of the two Muslims who have approached the Christian army with a white flag, evidently to parley. A bishop then tells the other messenger to tell his king that God will help the Christians win. The message is clear. Their war is just because God is with the Christians. The Muslims are infidels and therefore any action against them, even the most dreadful, is justifiable. A peaceful agreement with them is unthinkable. In the rest of the film Roland's actions aim both to prevent any attempt of pacification between Christians and Muslims and to intensify the conflict between them. Cassenti heightened the negativity of his Roland by showing his villainous face with strong contrasts of light and shadow.

FIGURE 3.3   Roland and his helmet (screenshot from *La Chanson de Roland*)

The provocative version of *The Song of Roland* also concerns the traitor Gano. Unlike the medieval character, the Gano of the 1970s is portrayed as an individual endowed with high moral qualities who sincerely wishes for peace with the Muslims. The director altered his figure to such an extent that in the scene in which the pilgrim actors are supposed to play the part about Gano's betrayal, the actor with the role of Gano collapses suddenly; one of his companions tells the spectators that 'he could never have played the moment in which Gano betrays', implicitly underlining that the Gano of the medieval *Song of Roland* was not the real one.

In the film there are many allusions to the modern struggles of the oppressed classes and to the widespread ideas expressed by Frantz Fanon, who in his 1961 book, *The Wretched of the Earth*, points out that the break with the past and the end of oppression could be achieved using any means, including violence, and that especially the exploited of the countryside had to implement this revolution. In the film, the pilgrims meet a group of peasants fleeing after rebelling against their lord. To show that contemporary women were also making their contribution against oppression, the leader of the rebels is a woman.

In addition to the fact that one had to fight the oppressors, their appearance introduces the importance of the oppressed becoming aware of the importance of collective values. That is the only way to be able to save all the oppressed and is opposed to the religious choice (the opium of the people for Marx) like the pilgrimage that aims at salvation through an individual path. The rebels therefore reject the invitation to join the pilgrims. However, the struggle for (secular) salvation is still in progress and is not without its defeats. Following the motto that our defeats will be our victories because even defeats serve to raise consciousness, shortly after the pilgrims and the peasants take two different paths, and the soldiers of some nobles kill the rebels.

The pilgrims continue their journey towards Santiago of Compostela, but Klaus, the actor playing the role of Roland, proves to have completely opposite values to those of the medieval Roland. In fact, he goes with two companions to Flanders to join the rebels there. For the moment the oppressors have won, but the fight against them continues.

In line with the principle that emerged strongly in the 1960s and particularly in the 1970s that even the subordinate classes must be considered as active subjects in history and it is legitimate to examine them, in the film the cleric intent on writing Roland's story also puts in writing the stories of the pilgrims, among whom, in addition to 'normal' people, there are symbols of the subordinate and exploited such as a former prostitute and a former slave from Africa. Klaus represents the illiterate subaltern whose 'class consciousness' and desire to fight against the oppressors are awakened thanks to education; in fact, he learns to read (famous in those years was the motto that the master was the master because he knew a thousand words, while the worker was the worker because he knew a hundred words). Just as the children of the pilgrims are surprised that their lives and those of the other pilgrims are not only written down, but put side by side with the deeds of the so-called great men of history, such an egalitarian spirit, unthinkable for the Middle Ages, may surprise professional medievalists but, as the director himself pointed out, the film is not about the past but about the present. It is not by chance that one reviewer defined the film as *The Song of Roland*'s French Communist Party way.

Militant and provocative transpositions

In the 1970s, Cassenti was not the only one to make a filmic transposition of a medieval literary text considered as a pillar of the culture of a European country with anti-systemic aims. In 1971, the Italian director and writer Pier Paolo Pasolini released his film *The Decameron*, based on some of the one hundred novellas collected in the homonymous work by Giovanni Boccaccio (1313–1375). The medieval writer narrated that in order to escape the 1348 plague, a group of young Florentines, seven women and three men, had taken refuge in the countryside where, to spend time and not think about what was happening in their city, they had decided to tell each other stories (most of them follow themes chosen from day to day) and reflect on their meaning. The topics are the praise of fortune and mercantile enterprise, unhappy and joyful loves, mockeries, and cases of magnificence and courtesy. Focused on the world of the laity, especially the middle classes of medieval Tuscany, the tales often celebrate the earthly values of the laity and mercilessly mock the hypocrisy and corruption of the churchmen. Most of them are set in Tuscany, but there are also stories that take place in the areas where Italian merchants were active in the fourteenth century (England, Flanders, France, and the Mediterranean basin).

Unlike the French director, Pasolini did not make any drastic modifications to the medieval text, but changed the general framework, language, and setting and made a well-targeted selection of the novellas. His first objective was to bring to the fore members of the so-called subaltern classes and to emphasize the vitality and relevance of their culture and world, a world that was about to be submerged by contemporary industrial civilization. In the film, the narrator and his audience do not belong to the privileged classes as in Boccaccio's *Decameron*, but are a street story-teller and commoners respectively. Their very 'normal' appearance (there are overweight and short people and bald and toothless men) emphasizes this characteristic.

Following the egalitarian spirit according to which we are and seem to be all equal, Pasolini also chose the novella in which it is told that the famous painter Giotto, surprised by a storm while he was traveling with a well-known expert in law, takes refuge with him in a hut. After changing their soaked clothes and putting on the poor clothes available there, the two start to laugh, thinking about what people would think seeing them in that state. Surely their clothes would not lead people to believe that they were famous men of high intellect. With great irony, the director played Giotto.

The narrator and the characters in the film do not speak in Tuscan vernacular but in an Italian with a strong Neapolitan accent, and all the stories take place in Naples or in other places in southern Italy (Pasolini used three novellas with a

Neapolitan setting and Neapolitanized the other tales that originally took place in central Italy; in one case, however, he Neapolitanized the characters whose events took place in northern Europe). In an interview, the director underlined that he had made this choice because

> Naples represents a historical reality that I like but that no longer exists. The Neapolitans have decided to remain what they were and thus to let themselves die.

In his vision Naples and its inhabitants therefore symbolize that world which was about to be eliminated from contemporary society. Putting Naples and the Neapolitans, often considered as the incarnation of the Mezzogiorno—the least developed part of contemporary Italy—at the center of a work that became a fundamental text for school education in contemporary Italy, undoubtedly reinforced this message. It cannot be excluded that this choice was also a criticism of the Tuscanization of the Italian language carried out after the unification of Italy in the nineteenth century, an operation that had given a subordinate role to Italian dialects, especially to those less similar to Tuscan—for example, those of the South—and had further accentuated the subordination of those using those dialects, that is, the less wealthy classes. Although Pasolini kept some of the tales with characters belonging to the middle and lower-middle classes, he gave a clear preference to those concerning members of the lower and the lower-middle classes and did not include novellas about the wealthy and 'high' culture.

Killing several birds with only one stone, many of those novellas also have the distinction of being among the most erotic of Boccaccio's work and of referring to hot topics such as premarital sex, adultery, and the lack of respect for chastity by some churchmen, and for this reason they were not (and still are not) included in the anthologies used in Italian schools. In addition to criticizing the hypocrisies inherent in the educational system, the joyful and vital eroticism of those stories was in line with the idea—widespread among young people of the counterculture and some intellectuals of the Left—that it was necessary to live and express sexuality in a more joyful and free way and therefore to oppose the constraints imposed by the morals of the Church and the ruling classes aimed at controlling the population.

Paradigmatic in this regard because they illustrate well the hypocrisy of such constraints that apply to the subordinate but not to the dominant are the novella about Lisabetta and a change made by Pasolini from the original. The story tells the sad tale of Lisabetta, a girl from a wealthy family, who dies of a broken heart because her brothers not only kill Lorenzo, one of their employees who dared to have an affair with her, but also they make the head of the boy disappear, which Lisabetta placed in a vase in order to continue to have her beloved with her. In order to accentuate the double moral of the males, Pasolini shows that the brother, who discovered the affair between Lisabetta and Lorenzo, was in bed with a woman. The director also changes the ending by omitting the disappearance of

Lorenzo's head and not having Lisabetta die, thus mitigating the defeat of the subordinate (see Boccaccio's story in primary source E).

More joyful and to the satisfaction of all the characters is, on the contrary, the novella of Masetto in which he makes fun of the double morality of some members of the Church. Pretending to be deaf and mute, Masetto, a handsome and robust young man, manages to be hired as a gardener in a nunnery where all the nuns have sex with him, thinking that they can keep this hidden thanks to Masetto's disability.

Particularly useful for Pasolini's objective is the fact that there are novellas in which there are women (whose sexuality patriarchal society always tried to control) who, unlike Lisabetta, manage to successfully enjoy sex outside of the norms imposed by society, and sometimes even manage to ridicule men. Peronella makes her not very clever husband, who has returned home earlier than expected, believe that her lover, hiding in a large jar, was there to inspect the container before buying it and that she could get a higher sum of money from the sale than her husband wanted to sell it for. The woman is also able to resume her activities with her lover because the latter tells the husband that he would not have bought it if its interior was not perfectly cleaned. Differing from the original text, the director accentuates the role of the woman to the detriment of the man by making Peronella incite her husband to clean with more energy, while in reality she invites her lover to get busy.

Caterina, a beautiful girl, manages to gull her father, who wanted to preserve his daughter's virginity until she would have found a husband he considered suitable. Not only does she manage to escape her parent's surveillance with a ruse and have sexual intercourse with her beloved, but she is able to marry him because, discovered by her father, the latter decides that the young man must marry Caterina if he does not want to be killed.

In line with the idea that everyone should have the right to express one's sexuality in any way, including positions considered sinful, there is the novella of the cunning priest peddler Gianni, who convinces a traveling salesman named Peter and his young and pretty wife Gemmata that he can transform the woman into a mare whom Peter could thus take with him. The magic rite implies that Gemmata undresses completely, that Gianni touches every part of the woman to make her become a mare and that nobody says a word during the ritual. The couple accepts, but the husband expresses his opposition when Gianni attaches the tail to Gemmata by penetrating her from behind, thus cancelling the transformation and losing the opportunity to have his wife with him in the long trips away from home. Both in Boccaccio's work and in the film it is not clear if the astute priest had anal sex with Gemmata. The uncertainty that he did so certainly favored the provocative goal of Pasolini who, being homosexual, probably appreciated the ambiguity of that detail.

It is no coincidence that the film ends with the story of two friends, Tingoccio and Meuccio who, worried about what would happen to them in the afterlife and frustrated by the fact that churchmen were rather vague about it, exchanged the promise that the first to die had to reveal to the one left on earth what happened after death. Pasolini intentionally changes the ending of the story where

Tingoccio, after dying, returns to earth reassuring Meuccio that it is not a sin to have sex with one's godfather's wife. Unlike Boccaccio's *Decameron*, where Meuccio regrets all the opportunities he let slip away, the director shows Meuccio rushing to his lover to tell her 'it's not a sin', a statement that sums up the film's main objective.

Pasolini carried out a similar operation with *The Canterbury Tales* (1972), a transposition of the homonymous text by the English writer Geoffrey Chaucer (c. 1340–1400), considered a cornerstone of English literature. In that work the author imagines meeting in a tavern in London twenty-nine pilgrims with whom he goes to Canterbury to honor the relics of Thomas Beckett. To make the journey less boring some of them tell short stories (twenty-four in total). Among the pilgrims there are both clergy and laypeople, and among the latter all classes (except the aristocracy and peasants) are represented. Their tales, on the other hand, concern all components of English society with a particular focus on the middle class. Chaucer organized the narrators and their tales according to his own well-determined scale of social and moral values ranging from top to bottom. The work begins with the knight, a person of high moral and social standing, and his tale of courtly love, and ends with the most abject character of the group, the indulgence seller with the story of the three friends who kill each other. Most of the stories are marked by humor that sometimes becomes satire of the behavior of churchmen and some members of the middle class.

Although less provocative than that carried out in *The Decameron*, in this film, too, Pasolini carries out a linguistic operation with social and cultural objectives. In the English version, the characters speak in the languages of the 'subordinates' of the modern United Kingdom, ranging from English with a Scottish accent to the London dialect of the working classes. In the Italian version, there is a mixture of regional Italian languages typical of certain areas of Lombardy and northeastern Italy. In order to reinforce its orientation towards the lower classes, the dubbing was not done by professional actors.

However, the characteristics of Chaucer's work did not allow the director to make a selection of stories that would bring the world of the lower classes to the forefront. Pasolini therefore had to focus on a different objective, namely the criticism of the clergy and middle-class values that are often implicitly praised by Chaucer. Except for the position of the seller of indulgences and his account, the director did not follow Chaucer's scale of moral and social values, thus implicitly pointing out that he did not want to attribute the objectives of the medieval work to the film.

The eight tales chosen by the director have above all the particularity of being the darkest of the *Canterbury Tales*, a darkness that Pasolini increased by choosing grey landscapes and permeating the film with long silences. Eros, symbol of vitality in the *Decameron*, in the transposition of Chaucer's tales often becomes synonymous with death. Death also pervades all the stories in the film. A funeral, a murder, a condemned man, and a dying man are described. It is no coincidence that Pasolini's selection includes a story in which death, in addition to being the destiny to which the characters are doomed, is itself a character (a thief called 'Death'). In addition to accentuating their disreputable behavior, the director criticizes the wealthy classes by emphasizing the unpleasant appearance of the characters belonging to that class through very heavy and vulgar makeup. Pasolini himself highlighted his desire to condemn 'bourgeois values' in some interviews.

> The *Canterbury Tales* were written forty years after the *Decameron* but the relations between realism and the fantastic dimension are the same, but Chaucer was coarser than Boccaccio; on the other hand the English writer was more modern, since a bourgeoisie already existed in England, as later in Cervantes's Spain. That is, there is already a contradiction: on the one hand the epic aspect with uncouth heroes full of vitality of the Middle Ages, on the other hand irony and self-mockery, essentially bourgeois phenomena and signs of bad conscience.

> Chaucer straddles two eras. It has something medieval, gothic: the metaphysics of death. But you often feel like you are reading an author like Shakespeare or Rabelais or Cervantes. He is a realist, but he is also a moralist and a pedant, and he also shows extraordinary insights. He still has one foot in the Middle Ages, but he is not one of the lower classes, although he takes his tales from popular culture. In essence, he is already a bourgeois. He already looks to the Protestant revolution and even the liberal revolution, to the extent that the two phenomena will combine in Cromwell. But while Boccaccio, who was also a bourgeois, had a quiet conscience, with Chaucer there is already an unpleasant feeling, a troubled and unhappy conscience. Chaucer foresees all the victories, all the triumphs of the bourgeoisie, but he is also aware of its rottenness. He is a moralist, but also endowed with a sense of irony.

Although Pasolini was often in controversy with the official positions of the Left, these statements reveal how much he was influenced by the pseudo-Marxist hasty literary and historical analyses that were quite widespread in the 1960s and the 1970s and that for their excessive schematisms provided a wrong idea of the past. Without going into lengthy disquisitions on the fact that the divisions into epochs are only conventions and on the enormous differences existing among the various parts of Europe and on the fact that almost all the positions of the Protestants were already present among the medieval heretics as well as the fact that the modern authors did not completely create new themes, it is necessary at least to observe that Tuscany and other parts of Italy in the late Middle Ages had a middle class just as developed (and in some cases much more) than Chaucer's England and that this knowledge was already acquired when Pasolini's films were released.

The director completed his operation on the classics of the medieval era with *The Flower of the One Thousand and One Nights* (1974) based on the collection of tales known as the *Arabian Nights*, a corpus of Middle Eastern stories created perhaps starting in the ninth/tenth century and growing over the centuries. In this case, Pasolini kept the theme of eroticism as a vital and natural force without, however, making any other cultural or social provocation.

With his films Pasolini undoubtedly distorted the original meaning of the medieval texts (very difficult to transpose into a film because of the large number of themes and tales), but he succeeded in achieving some of his objectives. His *Decameron* and *The Canterbury Tales* obtained the recognition of most of the critics, especially abroad (both won the first prize at the Berlin Film Festival), and the interest of a wide audience (especially the *Decameron*) and scandalized the moralists (public authorities seized the movies for a few months and the director was tried for outrage against public morals, a charge from which he was later acquitted). His 'anthropological' operation on the Neapolitans and the lower classes was probably understood only by some specialists of Boccaccio and Chaucer, and the importance given to the so-called erotic tales gave way to the popular genre of 'Boccaccio films', whose eroticism, while unconsciously conveying the will of a part of society eager to put an end to some hypocrisies and taboos of the past, was an end in itself.

Primary sources

A) *Francis sells his father's clothes and his horse and donates the money to a poor priest*

Francis rose, fortifying himself with the sign of the cross, and when his horse was ready he mounted. Taking some fine cloth with him, he rode to the city of Foligno. There, being a successful merchant, he sold all his cloth as usual and even left behind the horse he was riding, having received a good price for it. Then, having left all his baggage behind, he started back, wondering as he traveled what he should do with the money.

Soon, converted to God's work in a marvelous way, he felt it would be burdensome to carry the money for even an hour and, treating it as if it were sand, he decided to get rid of it as fast as possible. As he approached the city of Assisi, he passed the church built in honor of St. Damian long ago, but now about to collapse with age.

When the new soldier of Christ arrived at the church, he was stirred with pity for its condition and entered with fear and reverence. Finding a poor priest inside, Francis kissed his sacred hands and offered him the money he was carrying, telling the priest what he intended to do. The priest was stunned. Astonished by such an incredibly sudden conversion, he refused to believe what he heard. Since he thought he was being deceived, he refused to keep the money that had been offered him. He had seen Francis just the other day, so to speak, living riotously among his relations and acquaintances, acting even more stupidly than the rest.

Francis, stubbornly insistent, tried to prove he was sincere. He begged the priest to let him stay there for the sake of the lord. Finally the priest agreed that he could stay but, fearing Francis' parents, he would not accept the money. Francis, genuinely contemptuous of money, threw it on a window sill, treating it as if it were dust. He wanted to possess wisdom, which is better than gold, and prudence, which is more precious than silver.

Thomas of Celano, *First and Second Lives of Saint Francis,* translated by David Burr, available in https://sourcebooks.fordham.edu/source/stfran-lives.asp (accessed on September 22, 2021).

B) *The meeting with the pope*

Francis came to Rome with all his brothers, hoping that Pope Innocent III would confirm what he had written. At that time the venerable bishop of Assisi, Guido, who honored Francis and the brothers and prized them with a special love, also happened to be in Rome. When he saw Francis and his brothers there and did not know the cause, he was very upset, since he feared they were planning to desert their native city, in which God was now doing great things through his servants. . . .

Saint Francis also went to the bishop of Sabina, John of Saint Paul, one of the great members of the Roman court who seemed to despise earthly things and love heavenly ones. Receiving Francis with kindness and love, the bishop praised him highly for his request and intention.

Since he was a prudent and discreet man, the bishop began to question Francis about many things and tried to convince him that he should try the life of a monk or hermit. Saint Francis humbly refused his advice as well as he could, not because he despised what the bishop suggested but because, impelled by a higher desire, he devoutly wished for something else. The lord bishop marveled at his fervor and, fearing that he might eventually slip back from such high intentions, tried to show him a path that would be easier to follow. Finally, won over by Francis' constancy, the bishop agreed to his petition and attempted to further his plan before the pope.

At that time the Church was led by Innocent III, who was famous, very learned, gifted in speech, and burning with zeal for whatever would further the cause of the Christian faith. When he had discovered what these men of God wanted and thought the matter over, he assented to their request and did what had to be done. Exhorting and admonishing them about many things, he blessed Saint Francis and his brothers, saying to them, 'Go with the Lord, brothers, and preach penance to all as the Lord will inspire you. Then, when the Lord increases you in number and in grace, return joyously to me. At that time I will concede more to you and commit greater things to you more confidently.'

Thomas of Celano, *First and Second Lives of Saint Francis,* translated by David Burr, available in https://sourcebooks.fordham.edu/source/stfran-lives.asp (accessed on September 22, 2021).

C) *The meeting with the pope according to an English chronicler*

The Pope attentively considered the brother standing before him: his strange habit, his ignoble countenance, his long beard, his unkempt hair, and his dirty and overhanging brow, and once he had Francis's petition read, which was so difficult, indeed impossible in common estimation to carry out, he despised him and said: 'Go, brother, and look for some pigs, to whom you are more fit to be compared rather than to human beings, and roll around with them in a slough; give them this Rule you prepared and fulfill there your office of preaching.'

When Francis heard these words, he bowed his head and left immediately. He finally found some pigs and rolled with them in the mud until he had covered his body and habit with filth from head to toe. He then returned to the consistory and presented himself to the gaze of the Pope: 'My Lord', he said, 'I have done as you ordered; I beg you, now hear my petition.' When the astonished Pope saw what Francis had done, he deeply regretted having treated him with contempt. When he composed himself, he ordered Francis to wash himself and then return to him. Francis swiftly cleansed himself from the filth and returned immediately. Overcome with emotion because of this, the Pope granted his petition; after confirming his Order and, through a privilege of Roman Church, the office of preaching which he had requested, he dismissed him with a blessing.

The chronicle of Roger of Wendover, in *Francis of Assisi: Early Documents*, volume I, eds. R. J. Armstrong, J. A. W. Hellmann, W. J. Short (New York, 1999), pp. 598–99.

D) *Clare and Francis*

Hearing of the then celebrated name of Francis, who, like a new man was renewing with new virtues the way of perfection forgotten by the world, she was moved by the Father of the spirits . . . and immediately desired to see and hear him. . . .

With only one close companion accompanying her, the young girl, leaving her paternal home frequented . . . clandestine meetings with the man of God, whose words seemed to her to be on fire and whose deeds were seen to be beyond the human. . . .

He whispered in her ears of a sweet espousal with Christ, persuading her to preserve the pearl of her virginal purity for that blessed Spouse Whom Love made man. . . .

Immediately an insight into the eternal joys was opened to her at whose vision the world itself would become worthless, with whose desire she would begin to melt, for whose love she would begin to yearn for heavenly nuptials. . . .

Then she committed herself thoroughly to the counsel of Francis, placing him, after God, as the guide of her journey.

The Legend of Saint Clare (1254–1255), in *Clare of Assisi: Early Documents*, edited and translated by R. J. Armstrong (Saint Bonaventure, New York, 1993), pp. 256–58.

E) *Lisabetta and her lover and her brothers*

Know then that there were at Messina three young men, that were brothers and merchants, who were left very rich on the death of their father, who was of San

Gimignano; and they had a sister, Lisabetta by name, a girl fair enough, and no less debonair, but whom, for some reason or another, they had not as yet bestowed in marriage. The three brothers had also in their shop a young Pisan, Lorenzo by name, who managed all their affairs, and who was so goodly of person and gallant, that Lisabetta bestowed many a glance upon him, and began to regard him with extraordinary favour; which Lorenzo marking from time to time, gave up all his other amours, and in like manner began to affect her, and so, their loves being equal, it was not long before they took heart of grace, and did that which each most desired. Wherein continuing to their no small mutual solace and delight, they neglected to order it with due secrecy, whereby one night as Lisabetta was going to Lorenzo's room, she, all unwitting, was observed by the eldest of the brothers, who, albeit much distressed by what he had learnt, yet, being a young man of discretion, was swayed by considerations more seemly, and, allowing no word to escape him, spent the night in turning the affair over in his mind in divers ways. On the morrow he told his brothers that which, touching Lisabetta and Lorenzo, he had observed in the night, which, that no shame might thence ensue either to them or to their sister, they after long consultation determined to pass over in silence, making as if they had seen or heard nought thereof, until such time as they in a safe and convenient manner might banish this disgrace from their sight before it could go further. Adhering to which purpose, they jested and laughed with Lorenzo as they had been wont; and after a while pretending that they were all three going forth of the city on pleasure, they took Lorenzo with them; and being come to a remote and very lonely spot, seeing that it was apt for their design, they took Lorenzo, who was completely off his guard, and slew him, and buried him on such wise that none was aware of it. On their return to Messina they gave out that they had sent him away on business; which was readily believed, because it was what they had been frequently used to do. But as Lorenzo did not return, and Lisabetta questioned the brothers about him with great frequency and urgency, being sorely grieved by his long absence, it so befell that one day, when she was very pressing in her enquiries, one of the brothers said: 'What means this? What hast thou to do with Lorenzo, that thou shouldst ask about him so often? Ask us no more, or we will give thee such answer as thou deservest.' So the girl, sick at heart and sorrowful, fearing she knew not what, asked no questions; but many a time at night she called piteously to him, and besought him to come to her, and bewailed his long tarrying with many a tear, and ever yearning for his return, languished in total dejection.

But so it was that one night, when, after long weeping that her Lorenzo came not back, she had at last fallen asleep, Lorenzo appeared to her in a dream, wan and in utter disarray, his clothes torn to shreds and sodden; and thus, as she thought, he spoke: 'Lisabetta, thou dost nought but call me, and vex thyself for my long tarrying, and bitterly upbraid me with thy tears; wherefore be it known to thee that return to thee I may not, because the last day that thou didst see me thy brothers slew me.' After which, he described the place where they had buried him, told her to call and expect him no more, and vanished. The girl then awoke, and doubting not that the vision was true, wept bitterly. And when morning came, and she was risen, not daring to say aught to her brothers, she resolved to go to the place indicated in the vision, and see if what she had dreamed were even as it had appeared to her. So, having leave to go a little way out of the city for recreation in company with a maid that had at one time lived with them and knew all that she did, she hied her thither with all speed; and having removed the dry leaves that were strewn about the place, she began to dig where the earth seemed least hard. Nor had she dug long, before she found the body of her hapless lover, whereon as yet there was no trace of corruption or decay; and thus she saw without any manner of doubt that her vision was true. And so, saddest of women, knowing that she might not bewail him there, she would gladly, if she could, have carried away the body and given it more honourable sepulture elsewhere; but as she might not so do, she took a knife, and, as best she could, severed the head from the trunk, and wrapped it in a napkin and laid it in the lap of her maid; and having covered the rest of the corpse with earth, she left the spot, having been seen by none, and went home. There she shut herself up in her room with the head, and kissed it a thousand times in every part, and wept long and bitterly over it, till she had bathed it in her tears. She then wrapped it in a piece of fine cloth, and set it in a large and beautiful pot of the sort in which marjoram or basil is planted, and covered it with earth, and therein planted some roots of the goodliest basil of Salerno, and drenched them only with her tears, or water perfumed with roses or orange-blossoms. And it was her wont ever to sit beside this pot, and, all her soul one yearning, to pore upon it, as that which enshrined her Lorenzo, and when long time she had so done, she would bend over it, and weep a great while, until the basil was quite bathed in her tears.

Fostered with such constant, unremitting care, and nourished by the richness given to the soil by the decaying head that lay therein, the basil burgeoned out in exceeding great beauty and fragrance. And, the girl persevering ever in this way of life, the neighbours from time to time took note of it, and when her brothers marvelled to see her beauty ruined, and her eyes as it were evanished from her head, they told them of it, saying: 'We have observed that such is her daily wont.' Whereupon the brothers, marking her behaviour, chid her therefore once or twice, and as she heeded them not, caused the pot to be taken privily from her. Which, so soon as she missed it, she demanded with the utmost instance and insistence, and, as they gave it not back to her, ceased not to wail and weep, insomuch that she fell sick; nor in her sickness craved she aught but the pot of basil. Whereat the young men, marvelling mightily, resolved to see what the pot might contain; and having removed the earth they espied the cloth, and therein the head, which was not yet so decayed, but that by the curled locks they knew it for Lorenzo's head. Passing strange they found it, and fearing lest it should be bruited abroad, they buried the head, and, with as little said as might be, took order for their privy departure from Messina, and hied them thence to Naples. The girl ceased not to weep and crave her pot, and, so weeping, died. Such was the end of her disastrous love; but not a few in course of time coming to know the truth of the affair, there was one that made the song that is still sung: to wit:

A thief he was, I swear,
A sorry Christian he,
That took my basil of Salerno fair, etc.

The Decameron of Giovanni Boccaccio, translated by J. M. Rigg (London, 1903), fourth day, fifth story.

4

VIDEO RIGHT-WING AGENDAS

The previous chapter has shown that several filmmakers, favoring ideals and themes characteristic of the Left, have distorted history in their films in order to highlight the similarities between the past and the present and to raise public awareness about those topics. However, this operation has not only distinguished directors who are in favor of such ideas. In fact, there has been no lack of those who have produced movies that support exalted versions of patriotism and nationalism, demonize and reject the other, and justify and glorify the use of war. Unlike films with leftist themes, those with arguments typical of the Right did not have a golden age comparable to the 1960s and 1970s, but examples of them can be found from silent movies of the early decades of the twentieth century to a blockbuster of the early 2000s.

Fatherland, expansionism, and the invention of an exemplary past

The play *La Nave* (*The Ship*), by the famous Italian poet and writer Gabriele D'Annunzio (1863–1938), was staged with enormous success in 1908 and transposed to film in 1912 by Edoardo Bencivenga and in 1921 by Gabriellino D'Annunzio, Gabriele's son, and Mario Roncoroni. The plot is based on the events that, according to the movie, will lead to the creation of Venice.

In 552, on an island in the Venetian lagoon, where some inhabitants of the mainland had taken refuge to escape the barbarians, a conflict takes place between the members of the Gratico family, who embody the community's spiritual values—industriousness, courage, and desire for independence—and those of the Faledro family, who are eager to place the area under the rule of the Byzantine Empire. After being a puppet manipulated by the seductive dancer Basiliola Faledro, the leader of the Graticos emerges victorious and, to atone for the period in

DOI: 10.4324/9781003153139-5

which he forgot his values, decides to leave on a large ship to free the Adriatic Sea from the incursions of the Slavs.

Both the historical setting and the characters are fictional. In 552 the Byzantines were reconquering Italy, then still under the domination of the Ostrogoths, and some islands of the Venetian lagoon were inhabited, but there were never conflicts like those described in *The Ship*, and, following the Byzantine conquest of Italy, the lagoon area was under the rule of Constantinople until the eighth century. The surnames of the protagonists are not attested for that period of which almost nothing is known. That of Faledro was most likely chosen because in the fourteenth century the doge of Venice, Marin Falier, had tried to turn Venice into his personal dominion, thus becoming the Venetian traitor par excellence. The name Basiliola was instead invented because it indicated what she was; Basiliola in fact means little (Byzantine) empress (in Greek 'basilissa' means empress).

To those who do not know D'Annunzio and the historical contexts in which the play and the film were produced and seen, *The Ship* looks like an innocent story that, in addition to proposing another legend about the birth of Venice, shows a 'good guy' who, after many hardships, manages to win. It should first be remembered that at the beginning of the twentieth century in Italy there was a nationalist movement that, inspired by the exaltation of the superman and patriotism—also present in some of the works of Gabriele D'Annunzio—was pitted against the parliamentary governments because, it was argued, they were unable to bring out strong individuals capable of having a positive role for the entire nation. Therefore, on the one hand the nationalists harshly criticized the prudent domestic and especially foreign policy of the Italian government, accusing it of being mediocre, lacking in impetus, and blaming it for having created a 'little Italy' not in step with modern times. On the other hand, they advocated an aggressive foreign policy and a strong colonial expansionism that would allow Italy to put herself on par with the main European powers. In this regard it is necessary to remember that in their 1909 manifesto the Futurists, taking to extremes some of D'Annunzio's positions, stressed that war was the hygiene of the world. The strong desire for revenge after the defeats against Ethiopia at the end of the nineteenth century and the fact that a part of northeastern Italy was still under foreign rule helped to give strength to that movement, very popular especially among young educated people of the middle class. *The Ship* does not contain explicit messages, but the members of the nationalist movement and their sympathizers were ready to read between the lines and draw inspiration from the story of Mark Gratico, a military leader who, thanks to his strength of mind and personality, leads his community to victory.

More relevant, however, was the theme of the creation of Venice. The refusal of those ancient founding fathers to submit to a foreign power such as the Byzantine Empire had to be considered as a source of inspiration for modern Italians. The Byzantines were in fact the illegitimate heirs of the greatness and splendor of the Roman Empire and symbol par excellence of intrigue, decadence, debauchery, and mediocrity. The early Venetians' decision therefore allowed Venice to become one of the most shining examples of Italian history.

The departure of those ancient Venetians on a large ship, called 'Tutto il Mondo' (All the World), also invited modern Italians to think big and to undertake warlike enterprises. In 1908 the newspapers reported that at the end of the performances numerous spectators poured into the streets singing the leitmotif of *The Ship* at the top of their voices: 'Arm the stern and sail towards the world.' The reviewers were ready to catch the connections between D'Annunzio's work and the contemporary situation. One of them underlined that it was a patriotic poet's warning 'that looks beyond the miseries, the shame, the cowardice, the Byzantinisms of the current time', while another defined the play as 'a great breath of Italianness.'

Although the opinion of Carlo Sforza (Minister of Foreign Affairs in 1920– 1921) on D'Annunzio as the intellectual father of Fascism is influenced by hind- sight, it is noteworthy that in his memoirs published after World War II, he dwells precisely on *The Ship*, noting that

> the line 'arm the stern and sail to the world' seems innocent but, to students and young people yawning at the university or office, it seemed a program of greatness and war. . . . The Fascist mental corruption began then.

The periods in which the two films were released (1912 and 1921) were not only characterized by similar ideas, but also had the distinction of being marked by moments of strife. Suffice it to say that the first film appeared in movie theaters just as the war between Italy and the Ottoman Empire for the possession of Libya was ending, a conflict supported by an intense propaganda campaign. In those years, the nationalists observed that in this way the splendor of imperial Rome was revived.

For the other film it is not exaggerated to speak of an explosive context. To the heavy losses suffered by Italy in World War I were added the dissatisfaction with the results obtained despite Italy being among the winners (many spoke of a mutilated victory), a serious economic crisis, and the violent fights between leftists and fascists who took power by force in 1922. We do not know the background that led Gabriele D'Annunzio's son to make that film. It should be remembered, however, that when the Allies refused to grant Italy Dalmatia and the city of Fiume, on September 12, 1919, D'Annunzio occupied Fiume with rebellious Italian sol- diers (defined by the poet as legionaries in homage to the power of ancient Rome) and proclaimed its annexation to Italy. Under the threat of an intervention by the Italian army, D'Annunzio and his legionaries had to withdraw in December 1920; Fiume was proclaimed an independent state and almost all of Dalmatia was annexed to Yugoslavia.

Taking into account these details, it is relevant that in the 1921 film it is empha- sized on several occasions that the great ship, called 'All the World' in this film as well, represents the 'patria (fatherland)' and that, unlike in the play, where it is said that it was used to take away the relics of Saint Mark from Alexandria, in the film Mark Gratico embarks in that ship with the cream of the refugees to keep the Adriatic Sea safe from the Slavs, an enterprise very similar to that undertaken by the director's father between 1919 and 1920.

King Arthur in light of the American Red Scare

The Black Knight (1954) by US director Tay Garnett is very confusingly based on the deeds of the legendary King Arthur against Saxon invaders. For this study, the film is a valuable source because various characters and plot features clearly reflect the period in which it was made. Immediately following the end of World War II, the US government and many American conservatives became increasingly obsessed with Communist enemies who threatened their nation from both within and without. The fact that in 1945 the Congress Commission on Un-American Activities had become permanent, that in 1947 President Truman ordered all federal employees be monitored for loyalty to their nation, and that in the same year a law was enacted severely restricting the activities of labor unions and prohibiting Communists from holding union office well underscores the spread of such ideas. The atmosphere soon turned into paranoia in 1950, when Republican Senator Joseph McCarthy announced that he had lists of Communists infiltrating the highest levels of government and public administration. Although he never showed those lists, his denunciation started a series of investigations by the FBI and thousands of people lost their jobs because they were suspected of being supporters of the Soviet Union. The atmosphere became further heated as many were forced to provide information with the threat of being placed on those lists and being fired. The Red Scare also produced some trials against American citizens accused of being spies of the Soviet Union.

Like those of the early 1950s, the adversaries in the film are of two types, external and internal. The latter are the most devious and dangerous because, as McCarthy wanted to demonstrate, they lurk in the very heart of the government. In *The Black Knight* the traitor is in fact Palamides, one of the knights of the Round Table, the cream of King Arthur's faithful, whose task is to advise the sovereign and defend the kingdom from enemies. Just like many of the 'enemies' created by the Red Scare, Palamides is a newcomer, i.e. a foreigner, and not being a native he has therefore not been able to absorb and appreciate the high ideals on which Arthur's kingdom is based. There is also no shortage of allusions to his ambiguous sexuality. When he takes off his armor, Palamides wears flashy jewelry and uses cosmetics on his face. In short, he is portrayed as a deviant both mentally and physically, and accordingly nothing good can be expected from such a character.

It is no coincidence that Palamides is allied with another internal adversary, in theory a faithful ally of Arthur, King Mark, who in the film is still pagan, similar therefore to the godless, red, and false Americans of McCarthy's time. Like the latter, Mark's plan aims both to destroy Arthur's palace and to eradicate Christianity from his kingdom and create a people 'united beyond belief.' In this regard with the obvious goal of emphasizing the otherness of the external enemies, they are not the still pagan Saxons of Arthurian legends, but the Saracens, i.e. Muslims. Non-specialists of medieval history are reminded that the Arthurian legend is set in episodes that took place in the fifth century AD, that Mohammed converted the Arabs to Islam in the seventh century and that the Muslims never attacked England. On this point, it is, however, necessary to mention the fact that in a fifteenth century text the adversaries of Arthur are the Saracens.

Of course, in the film the good guys do not stand by and watch. However, the adversary acts from within, and as in early 1950s America, it is necessary to infiltrate them. With a statement worthy of one of McCarthy's recruiting agents, an Arthurian loyalist assigns blacksmith John the task of spying on the enemies: 'There is treason all about us and it must be stamped out before all of us.' It is noteworthy that, in keeping with all modern spy missions that operate outside the law, John is reminded that if he is captured, King Arthur will claim to know nothing about him and his mission.

The film was so connected to the atmosphere of the period in which was made that it inevitably followed the fate of the Red Scare and its main proponent. About a month after its release, McCarthy, who had begun to extend his investigations into untouchable and upstanding sectors (the military and implicitly President Dwight Eisenhower himself), was publicly condemned by US senators for his reprehensible conduct that had led the Senate 'into dishonor and disrepute.' McCarthy's political career ended and *The Black Knight* was a box office disaster and went down in history as one of the worst films about the Middle Ages.

A medieval hero and an agenda (unconsciously?) favorable to a Spanish dictator

Directed by US director Anthony Mann and shot in Spain (the producer was an American resident in that country), *El Cid* (1961) tells the story of the Spanish nobleman Rodrigo Diaz de Bivar (d. 1102), better known as El Cid. At the time of Rodrigo Diaz, the Iberian Peninsula, most of which had been conquered by Muslims at the beginning of the eighth century, was no longer marked by the presence of a powerful and wealthy Islamic state. In fact, it was divided into numerous Muslim principalities, often fighting among themselves and against the Christian potentates of the North of the Peninsula, that on several occasions were made tributary to the Christians of the North. The situation became even more complicated towards the end of the eleventh century when the Almoravids arrived in Spain from northwest Africa. Proponents of an uncompromising Islamism, they occupied the Iberian Muslim principalities and blocked the Christians' advance towards the south, inflicting a heavy defeat on them. Like other enterprising Christian warriors, El Cid took advantage of the chaotic political situation prior to the arrival of the Almoravids by serving with Islamic and Christian rulers and fighting against their enemies regardless of their faith (see primary source A). He finally crowned the dream of such adventurers by creating his own domain in Valencia, a city he had taken from his Muslim employer.

The real Rodrigo, whose story can be reconstructed thanks to Muslim and Christian narrative sources composed shortly after his death, certainly did not embody the qualities of the all-in-one hero. He could not, therefore, be used as the hero of a successful film; there were too many grey areas in this medieval adventurer. However, the screenwriter and director of *El Cid* did not have to completely invent a new El Cid. Their character was in fact largely taken from a medieval poem of the thirteenth century, where references to Rodrigo as a military entrepreneur in the pay of the highest bidder, including Muslims, do not appear and in which the protagonist is presented as an upright hero intent on fighting Muslims and Christian villains.

To a viewer unaware of contemporary Spanish history, the film appears as an inoffensive blockbuster based on a hero from the past where it is clear who the good guys and the bad guys are. The more educated spectators may see it as an almost complete transposition of a medieval epic poem. Yet for those familiar with the recent history of that country, some parts of the film take on propagandistic tones in favor of the Spanish dictator Francisco Franco (1892–1975), who in 1936 was placed at the head of those opposing the democratically elected government comprising Socialists, Communists, and anarchists. The clashes soon degenerated into a full-fledged civil war that caused about a million deaths, in which Italy, Germany, the Soviet Union as well as members of left-wing parties and associations from other nations participated more or less directly with volunteers and logistical aid. The conflict ended in 1939 with the victory of the insurgents and the creation of Franco's dictatorship.

During the civil war, General Franco created an image for himself that would cover up the fact that he was, after all, a soldier who rebelled against a legitimate government. In addition to emphasizing that God had given him the task of leading a crusade against a crazed and godless enemy, Franco presented himself as a new heroic El Cid who would defend Spain from its new adversaries. A few months after the insurrection, Franco's supporters brought out the first issue of a nationalist magazine entitled *Mio Cid* (My Cid) whose purpose was to raise El Cid's banners throughout Spain to be in line with 'his cause, his spirit and his example.' This was followed by the publication of a collection of ballads where the rebellious general was explicitly equated with El Cid. In a film about the 'liberation' of Barcelona, the heart of the Spanish Republicans, Franco is called 'Caesar, Cid and Alexander (the Great).'

References to El Cid continued even after the Civil War. In the Military Historical Institute, the Spanish dictator ordered the creation of a mural in which he is portrayed as a medieval warrior. In July 1955, during the ceremony for the dedication of a statue of El Cid he emphasized the similarities between medieval and modern Spain.

> The great service of our crusade, the virtue of our movement, is to have awakened an awareness of what we were, of what we are, and what we can be.

El Cid, according to Franco, was to be the symbol of the new Spain because

> in him is enshrined all the mystery of the great Spanish epics: service in noble undertakings, duty as norm, struggle in the service of the true God.

Whether the Spanish government had any role in creating the plot of the film cannot be determined. Franco certainly appreciated it greatly because he provided considerable logistical help to the production of the film whose premiere took place in the capital of Spain. The Spanish dictator did not attend only for security reasons (a few days earlier there had been an attempt on his life).

It is striking, however, that one of the most obvious similarities with Franco and the civil war in *El Cid* concerns some details not mentioned in the medieval poem. In fact, the film does not portray El Cid as a bitter enemy of the Muslims. On one occasion he liberates the emir of Zaragoza who then reciprocates the generosity of the Christian leader by fighting at his side (in reality El Cid was in the service of that Muslim lord). Franco had begun his military career in the Spanish Foreign Legion stationed in the Spanish protectorate in Morocco and largely composed of Muslim soldiers under the orders of Spanish officers. It was with these troops that Franco started his rebellion against the Republican government. During the civil war, his personal guard, the Guardia Mora, was made up of Moroccans dressed in white just like the 'good' Muslims in the film who fight alongside El Cid (image 4.1). Franco was so attached to them that on the first of October 1936, he arrived in the main square of Salamanca to receive the investiture as head of the Spanish state escorted by the Guardia Mora on horseback. This episode is very similar to the scene in the film in which El Cid enters Valencia accompanied by the 'good' Muslims.

FIGURE 4.1 The Guardia Mora of Franco (screenshot from a documentary)

It should be remembered that Franco did not use the Moors only for the effect they made in the parades and often assigned the Moroccan troops the task of rounding up and summarily executing his opponents. For those who had lived during the civil war, which ended only twenty-two years before the release of the film, those 'good' Muslims dressed in white certainly reminded them of the Guardia Mora and the Moroccan troops. For Franco and his supporters, their presence in the film probably constituted an appreciated recognition of the positive role they had played in the conflict. To those who had sided with the legitimate republican government that reference most likely turned their stomachs.

Sex, lies, and a white supremacist video agenda

A transposition of the homonymous graphic novel by the US cartoonist Frank Miller, *300* by the US director Zack Snyder tells the story of the Spartan King Leonidas, who for a few days in 480 BCE, with three hundred Spartan warriors and a contingent formed by other Greeks, blocked the huge army of the Persian ruler Xerxes at Thermopylae, a narrow canyon located in northeastern Greece, the crossing of which was necessary to invade Greece. Thanks to a traitor, however, the Persians managed to bypass the defensive line of the Greeks. Unlike their allies, Leonidas and his men refused to retreat and fought to the death.

At that time the Spartans had the best and most disciplined infantry in the Mediterranean and the Middle East. Because their city was far from the coast, they, unlike many Greeks, could not become rich and powerful using the opportunities offered by sea trade, but managed to emerge as one of the major powers of Greece by investing all their resources in military force. To achieve this, they created a system according to which the Spartiates—the only inhabitants of Sparta to have full rights—had to devote all their time to military training and warfare and put the welfare and protection of the community before any other personal interest, including family.

Their training began at birth. Infants were inspected by the authorities, and deformed babies and those deemed frail and sickly were eliminated. At the age of seven, children were taken away from their families, accustomed to living with their companions, and subjected to harsh physical and psychological training. Those who could not resist fell into disgrace and either committed suicide or left Sparta. To teach them that the community came before their families, they had to address adults as their fathers. At the age of nineteen they were admitted into the army and at thirty they acquired the right to be part of the assembly of the Spartiates and to form a family to live with in a private home. However, they had to continue their military service until the age of sixty. To reinforce the spirit of equality and camaraderie, the Spartiates were to take meals all together.

To allow them to devote themselves exclusively to military training and warfare, their maintenance was ensured by the labor of the semi-free, the Perieci, and especially of the slaves, the Ilotes, who belonged to the entire community and constituted the majority of the inhabitants of Sparta. To emphasize the inferiority and diversity of the Ilotes, the Spartiates often humiliated them and once a year declared war on them and could kill them with impunity. A relevant component of the training of Spartan boys—a sort of rite of passage during which they learned to kill a man—consisted in going out at night armed only with a dagger and killing as many Ilotes as possible.

In the fifth century BCE, Sparta was an oligarchy in which power was mainly in the hands of a council of twenty-eight members who were over sixty years old and were elected for life by the general assembly of all Spartiates. Each year this institution chose some magistrates, the ephors ('the overseers') whose task was to monitor the behavior of their fellow citizens and to propose laws. There were also two kings who, however, only performed the function of military leaders under the control of the ephors.

In 480, at the news that the Persian King Xerxes's army was approaching their lands with a huge army, the Greeks decided to face their enemies at Thermopylae, a pass between a mountain and the sea, consisting of a narrow gorge that allowed the passage of only one chariot at a time and was placed on the only road leading from the north to central Greece. The Greeks would have been able so to annul the numerical superiority of their adversaries. In that period there were the religious festivities called Carnee and the Olympic Games and, since the members of the coalition of the Greek city-states believed that the clashes at Thermopylae would have lasted long, they preferred to celebrate those festivities and to send to Thermopylae a vanguard of some thousand warriors. The bulk of the Greek army would have reached them later. The Spartans followed such a line of behavior and, to prove their commitment in that fight, were the first ones to send a small contingent (three hundred men at the command of their King Leonidas).

Thanks to the narrow space of Thermopylae and the perfect military organization and the courage of the Spartans (the other Greeks gave their contribution taking turn with the warriors of Leonidas in the front line), all the assaults of the army of Xerxes failed. Hoping to obtain a large reward, an inhabitant of that area, named Ephialtes, however, revealed to the Persians the existence of a path that led beyond Thermopylae. Knowing that the enemy was about to take them from behind, Leonidas advised his allies to leave and decided to stay with his men and fight to the death. According to the Greek historian Herodotus (c. 490–c. 420 BCE), the main source of this episode (see primary source B), the king took that decision to leave 'a glorious memory of himself, without affecting the prosperity of Sparta' and to ensure that the glory was reserved only for the Spartans. In this way Leonidas would have also fulfilled the verdict of the oracle consulted before going to Thermopylae, according to which either Sparta would have been destroyed by the Persians or its king would have died.

Surrounded by a huge number of Persians, the Spartans and other Greeks who refused to retreat fought to the last man. The Persians then moved south and reached Athens, which was set ablaze, but their fleet was shortly thereafter beaten by Greek ships at Salamis. For fear that the news of the defeat provoked revolts in his empire Xerxes returned to his capital leaving his troops in Greece. These troops, however, were routed by the Greeks under the command of the Spartan King Pausanias in 479. Shortly after this victory, the Greek ships inflicted another heavy defeat to what remained of the Persian fleet and Xerxes had therefore to give up his aims in Greece.

Released in 2006, the film follows the main plot of the graphic novel (published in 1998) and amplifies its racist messages, and, in the parts added by the director—and perhaps also by the cartoonist who collaborated on the screenplay—there are many references to the US invasion of Iraq in 2003.

Snyder first of all creates a visual link between the majority of the American audience he is addressing, that is, the white descendants of the emigrants from Central and Northern Europe, and the Spartans by having actors whose appearance is similar to that audience play the role of the latter. He does not go so far as to use blond people (some have light brown hair), but characters with Mediterranean features, i.e. like those of the Greeks, are completely absent. Snyder also invites that audience to identify the three hundred companions of King Leonidas, the cream of the Spartan army, with the Marines, the cream of the US army, making the former use on several occasions the typical incitement scream of the latter. This analogy takes on particular significance in the scene where, shortly after leaving Sparta, Leonidas and his men meet some Greeks from other cities eager to fight the Persians along with the Spartans. To the surprise of their leader that Leonidas has so few soldiers, the Spartan king replies by asking three of those Greeks what their profession was; they reply to be a potter, a sculptor, and a blacksmith. Then Leonidas asks his men what their profession is and they reply by shouting that war cry three times. Leonidas then notes that he has brought more warriors than the Greek leader has.

In the context of the war in Iraq, this affirmation concerning a very distant past assumes a relevant meaning also for the beginning of the third millennium. Like what had happened in Antiquity to the coalition of Greeks, the only country among the nations present in Iraq to maintain order after 2003 that could boast of having real soldiers, indeed the best soldiers in the world, was the United States. Just as in the movie, where the Greek allies are referred to as 'brave amateurs', the allied troops could be useful but not as crucial as the US troops.

This is not the only analogy between the past and the contemporary situation. First of all, the director does not simply create a clear difference between the 'good guys' and the 'bad guys' on which we will return later, but he structures the plot of the film to highlight who among the Spartans was in the right and who behaved in a way that was not only wrong but also highly reprehensible. Considering that the invasion of Iraq in 2003 did not have the approval of either the UN or the majority of the Western world and that, after the initial and quick success, the presence of the Americans and their allies in Iraq had to face a growing opposition, Snyder makes a very bad portrait of all the Spartans who declared their opposition to the war against the Persians.

First of all, the negative image of the latter and the clear difference between them and those who were in the right, namely Leonidas and his warriors, is expressed visually. Unlike the latter, the opponents of the Spartan king look horrible (the Spartan priests, whom the narrative voice defines as 'more creatures than men' emphasizing that their souls are blacker than hell) or are not manly and have a devious expression (the politician Theron, an invention of the director). Ephialtes, the traitor who causes the death of Leonidas and his men, revealing to the Persians how to take their opponents from behind, is a Spartan with horrible features. It is no coincidence that such a monster, both physically and morally, should not have existed. Since he was born deformed, according to Spartan laws he should have been killed immediately, but his parents saved him by fleeing with him from Sparta. The director also clearly shows that the opposition to the use of the army to block the attack of the Persians by the Spartan priests and Theron is not motivated by ideals, but by the fact that they have been corrupted by the enemy. Immediately after denying Leonidas permission to lead the army against the Persians, the priests receive a large amount of coins from a Persian emissary who promises them that his lord will make their shrine rich and famous (a hint to this is present in the graphic novel).

In the scene in which Leonidas's wife, Queen Gorgo, reacts to Theron's infamous accusations of having used her body to manipulate the decisions of the Spartan councilors by killing him in front of the Spartan assembly, a large number of coins with the effigy of the Persian ruler are seen coming out of Theron's robes, a detail showing everyone that he had been bribed by the enemy. This was evident from the beginning of the film where Theron appears next to the Persian emissary handing over a large amount of gold to the priests for speaking out against Leonidas's war plan. The director insists on the sordidness of this character by showing him as an unscrupulous politician. To the queen who asks for his support, Theron replies that he owns the Spartan Council, alluding in this way to the fact that he had bought the councilors.

In line with this process of vilification of the Spartan opponents, Snyder ascribes to them sexual behaviors outside the norm aimed at arousing the aversion of the spectators toward them. Theron does not limit himself to the reprehensible request to have sexual intercourse with Queen Gorgo if she wants to have his support, but he sodomizes her and is so sadistic that he tells her that 'it won't be short and it won't be pleasant at all.' In this way the director also shows that, unlike the brave Spartan warriors, politicians do not act by looking their opponents in the face but by hitting them from behind. In a scene worthy of a soft b-series porn movie, a beautiful teenage girl, very unclothed and clearly under the influence of drugs or alcohol (obviously she does not look Mediterranean at all), plays the role of oracle of the gods to determine whether they were for or against the use of the Spartan army against the Persians. After a dance with unnatural movements, the girl says a cryptic phrase that a priest interprets as he licks her (such details are absent in the graphic novel).

Significantly, this part ends by showing an emissary of Xerses who gives money to the priests and promises them fame and further riches. The scene in which Xerses convinces the deformed Spartan to betray the Spartans by offering him prestigious positions, money, and women is characterized by the presence of numerous half-naked women who, with gestures and lascivious poses, make Ephialtes understand what pleasures they can offer him if he accepts the proposal of the Persian ruler.

It is necessary to remember that all these characters and what they do are an invention. As indicated in the historical excursus and in the source placed in the appendix, the Spartan priests never opposed the war against the Persians, they did not perform such rituals and even less used half-naked girls as oracles; moreover the ephors were magistrates, not priests. Ephialtes was neither a Spartan nor a deformed man. Not only did an individual like Theron never exist, but in Sparta professional politicians like that character were unthinkable. All adult men had to serve in the army and only those over sixty could become members of the council. These inventions are narrative devices whose purpose is to indicate who the 'bad guys' were and how they behaved.

Snyder shows that he is not a puritanical prude who uses sex exclusively to condemn. It is no coincidence that immediately after the scene about the teenager exploited by the Spartan priests, we see how those who are in the right have sex. In fact, Leonidas has a 'healthy' sexual relationship with his wife during which the couple engages in giving and receiving pleasure in various, but not scandalous, positions. This part is also extremely relevant because, immediately before engaging in healthy sex with her husband, the queen tells Leonidas, who is discouraged by the priests' prohibition to fight the Persians and uncertain how to act.

> It is not a question of what a Spartan citizen should do . . . instead ask yourself what a free man should do.

The next morning Leonidas goes to fight the Persians with the three hundred most valiant Spartan warriors. Laws and prohibitions therefore do not apply if a free man acts rightly. And in the film this right action means using weapons to defend freedom, a concept repeated on numerous occasions. It should be remembered that even this detail is completely invented and that for the ancient Spartans respect for the law was the very essence of being Spartan.

Returning to the film, it is necessary to turn our attention to how the actions of Leonidas are opposed to those of Theron in a dialogue between the latter and Queen Gorgo who tries to get his support so that the army is sent to the rescue of Leonidas and his companions. 'This is politics not war. Leonidas is an idealist', Theron says and she answers: 'I know your kind. You send men to slaughter for your gain.' One who refuses diplomacy and thinks that war is the only way to solve the situation is not only right, but also an idealist. One who instead wants to follow politics is in the wrong and moreover is a person who thinks only of his own interests even if this requires the death of his compatriots.

Evident are the analogies with the period in which the film was shot. Just as Leonidas and his warriors do in the film, for the Americans and their allies invading Iraq and keeping it under military occupation had been a just action, morally irreproachable, and marked by noble ideals. Their objective had in fact been to defend freedom. In this regard it is worth remembering that shortly after the invasion of Iraq the Americans failed to find the weapons of mass destruction and to provide an ideal motivation to that war operation that was proving extremely bloody and expensive, both the US administration and the media in its favor began to insist more and more that the American Army was in Iraq to defend the freedom of the Western world and bring freedom to the Iraqis.

Queen Gorgo's words also refer to beliefs that are widespread among the most radical part of American conservatives. For them, individual freedom is superior to laws that can be transgressed if one believes to be right and to act as a free man. Therefore, the lack of support of the United Nations and other governments in the name of the rules of international law was harmful. It is no coincidence that the film also aims to demonize, and thus delegitimize, all those who were against the use of force and preferred to resort to politics and diplomacy.

The director provides further legitimacy to Leonidas's behavior by sacralizing his death. Surrounded by his enemies, who managed to get around the canyon defended by the Spartans, Leonidas and his men refuse to surrender and submit to the Persians and are then killed by their arrows. When the cloud of Persian darts ceases, the camera goes upwards and you can see that the bodies of the Spartan warriors form a circle at the center of which there is that of their king. The camera then zooms in on Leonidas, showing his corpse in a position similar to that of Christ on the cross (Leonidas assumes the same pose when the arrows are about to hit him). Like Christ who sacrificed himself to save all humankind, Leonidas sacrificed himself to save the freedom of the Greeks from the Persian tyrant.

FIGURE 4.2 Leonidas like Christ (screenshot from *300*)

Since the battle of Thermopylae took place about five hundred years before the birth of Christ, that reference and that symbolism are obviously anachronistic. However, it seems clear that Snyder is not interested in the past, but in the present. Appealing to the mindset of American viewers, for whom there is no contradiction between an aggressive use of force and Christianity—a religion theoretically strongly characterized by non-violence—the director gives a sacred dimension to Leonidas's actions to reinforce the idea that the Spartan king acted correctly and was inspired by morally and religiously irreproachable principles. Given the many similarities with the period in which the film was shot, it is not absurd to believe that Snyder wanted to emphasize that the same thing had happened with the war in Iraq.

An idealization of the Spartans also occurs in the scenes based on the daily life of the inhabitants of Sparta portrayed as a community of peaceful and hardworking people. In these scenes, people resembling the Ilotes, who constituted the majority of Sparta's inhabitants and were the only ones working, never appear, evidently because any mention of them would have compromised the idyllic image of peace and freedom that the director wanted to convey (this absence also characterizes the graphic novel).

In line with this desire to hide the brutal details of Spartan society and at the same time to glorify its martial aspects, there is the scene of the rite of passage of the young Leonidas who, in order to prove that he was a man and could become king, had gone out at night alone outside the city and had killed a huge wolf (this is also mentioned in the graphic novel). This episode is not only invented, but it also distorts and glorifies an extremely brutal reality; as it has already been explained, the rite of passage of the Spartan boys consisted in killing at night all the Ilotes they met.

In the film and in Miller's work, the adversaries are obviously the opposite of the heroic Spartans. Unlike the latter, their elite troops, the Immortals, do not hesitate to massacre unarmed civilians of all ages and both sexes, proving also to be extremely cruel and sadistic. Before reaching Thermopylae, the Spartans come across a Greek village in flames, whose inhabitants had all been hung from a tree according to a chilling composition. It is noteworthy that the only survivor of the massacre is a child who, not coincidentally, is the character with the lightest skin and hair in the entire film (this whole part is absent in the graphic novel). The enemy of that time is therefore similar to the one of the present who kills innocent civilians through bloody attacks with powerful explosives, and the victims of the fifth century BCE resemble those of the beginning of the third millennium.

The similarities between the past and the present continue in the scenes of the clashes between the three hundred and the Persians. As long as the Persians confront the Spartans by attacking them from the front, their numbers and the use of special armaments (an armored rhinoceros, elephants, a monstrous giant, and hand grenades) are useless. Nothing can overcome the courage, military organization, and esprit de corps of the three hundred (i.e. the Marines of Antiquity). The enemy achieves some success only when they strike treacherously, i.e. from behind. Immediately after having shown great heroism and formidable warrior skills, the young son of the Spartan commander is killed by a Persian who suddenly appeared behind him from a cloud of smoke (a scene not mentioned in Miller's work). This was exactly what was happening when the film was shot and appeared in movie theaters. American soldiers and their allies were not dying from face-to-face confrontations with their opponents but from their guerrilla operations, sniper fire, and bombings.

The Immortals are to such an extent portrayed as the opposite of the three hundred that they are shown as non-men (a theme already introduced at the beginning of the film where the advancing Persian army is compared to an approaching beast; it is also referred to as a monster). They wear masks that make them look like monkeys and cover horrible faces. Their weapons and uniforms give them the appearance of ninja warrior animals (image 4.3) and the narrator's voice describes them in this way: 'eyes as dark as night, teeth filed to fangs, soulless.' The enemy is thus dehumanized and takes on the appearance of a video game adversary, against whom one can do anything, including exterminating them without any remorse and using their bodies as material to build a defensive wall.

FIGURE 4.3 The Immortals in *300* (screenshot from *300*)

All this can appear as a naive visual gimmick. Although these peculiarities are hinted at in the graphic novel, which dates back to 1998, the images of the adversaries and the use of their bodies take on a sinister meaning when one considers what happened between 2003 and 2004 in the American prison of Abu Ghraib (Iraq). Some US prison guards amused themselves by creating piles of completely naked Iraqi prisoners and having themselves photographed with them; the 'trophy' photos were put on the Internet and were widely circulated (unfortunately, it cannot be determined whether those 'pranksters' read Miller's graphic novel). In the United States, the episode caused a bit of a scandal among the Democrats, was attributed to a few 'bad apples' belonging to the lower ranks of the army, and was quickly put to rest. There were other priorities. Bombings, guerrilla operations, and snipers were claiming more and more victims among American soldiers and it was not possible to undermine their morale and compromise their image with the public at home with such trifles.

Finally, there is another theme that, while not related to the war in Iraq, is connected to ideas that characterize many American conservatives. The graphic novel conveys racist messages, which are amplified in the film by having dark-skinned people play the role of most of the emissaries and generals of the Persian ruler (image 4.4). These representatives of evil are therefore

THIS IS SPARTA! Leonid and the Persian diplomat.300 Spartans. 2007.

2:00 / 4:29

FIGURE 4.4   Ambassador of Xerses (screenshot from *300*)

from sub-Saharan Africa, a detail that historically does not make any sense because the Persian empire did not have possessions in that part of Africa. It is not impossible that the Persians owned dark-skinned slaves yet it is highly unlikely that sub-Saharan Africans could have attained prominent positions in that empire.

Miller's and Snyder's goal is obviously not historical accuracy, but to use the mind-sets of their intended audience to make their message clear. Just think of the scene in the film in which, immediately after the Spartan priests had denied Leonidas permission to lead the army against the Persians, a dark-skinned man appears and hands them a large amount of money bearing the effigy of Xerses and promises them fame and riches for siding with the Persian ruler. The light quickly dims and the camera takes a close-up of the face of the emissary who bursts out in an evil laugh and whose eyes only remain visible. The bad man of the fairy tales, the bogeyman, is therefore a real man and he is black. Also the majority of the women of the court of Xerses who with lascivious and winking poses promise infinite carnal pleasures to Ephialtes if he accepts to side with the Persian sovereign have dark skin (this part is reported only in the film). In one case, the director portrays one of the black-skinned Persian commanders with large mustache and sideburns worthy of the worst caricature of a Mexican.

FIGURE 4.5 Emissary of Xerses with mustache (screenshot from *300*)

In general, the Persian warriors have a Middle Eastern physiognomy, but sometimes some of the warriors resemble individuals who would look good in a B-movie about Latin American gangsters (these details are absent in the graphic novel). The physiognomy of the enemies' leader is noteworthy. The actor who plays Xerses has Latin American origins, and in the film the Persian ruler is portrayed as a bizarre crossbreed (a reference to this is also found in the graphic novel) (image 4.6). He is very tall and has a metallic voice, but at the same time he always has heavy make-up, piercings, lots of jewels all over his body, and full lips and woman's eyes on which the camera lingers while he tries to convince Leonidas and Ephialtes to join him.

The enemy therefore summarizes all the connotations of what many American conservatives despise and consider a danger to their world: African Americans, Latinos, mestizos, and people of ambiguous appearance and sexuality. Taking into account these details and the context in which the film was shot, the location of Thermopylae, situated on the border of Greece, takes on a highly symbolic meaning for the present as well. All those who are different from white Westerners must in fact be prevented in any way from entering the Western world and especially the United States.

FIGURE 4.6   Xerses (screenshot from *300*)

Primary sources

A) *El Cid at the service of Muslim rulers*

Chapter 7, pp. 102–03. When Rodrigo Diaz came to al-Mu'tamid he was at once told that the king of Granada with his Christian allies was advancing upon Mu'tamid and his kingdom. So he sent letters to the king of Granada and to the Christians who were with him, requesting them for the love of their lord King Alfonso not to come against the king of Seville nor to enter his kingdom. But they, trusting in the great size of their army, not only refused to listen to his requests but even altogether rejected them. Instead they advanced laying waste all the land as far as the castle known as Cabra. . . . When Rodrigo Diaz heard and checked the truth of this, he at once went out with his army to confront them. A hard-fought battle took place, lasting from the third hour of the day until the sixth. The army of the king of Granada, both Saracens and Christians, suffered very great carnage and casualties. Eventually, defeated and disordered, all fled from the face of Rodrigo Diaz.

Chapter 12, p. 105. Rodrigo gave his allegiance to al-Muqtadir of Zaragoza, who received him with great honour and treated him with much respect. While Rodrigo was residing contentedly at Zaragoza, al-Muqtadir fell ill and died. His realm was divided between his two sons, al-Mu'tamin and al-Hayib: al-Mu'tamin reigned in Zaragoza, his brother al-Hayib in Denia. This al-Mu'tamin was very fond of Rodrigo and set him over and exalted him above all his kingdom and all his land, relying upon his counsel in all things. A dreadful and most bitter quarrel broke out between al-Mu'tamin and his brother al-Hayib, and they agreed a time at which they might do battle together. Now Sancho, king of Aragon and Pamplona, and Berenguer, count of Barcelona, accompanied al-Hayib as his allies. With al-Mu'tamin was Rodrigo Diaz, who served him faithfully and guarded and protected his kingdom and land.

Historia Roderici, in *The World of El Cid: Chronicles of the Spanish Reconquest*, translated and annotated by S. Barton and R. Fletcher (Manchester, 2000).

B) *The battle of Thermopilae*

Chapter 175. The counsel that prevailed was, that they should guard the pass of Thermopylae; for the Greeks saw that it was narrower than the pass into Thessaly. . . .

Chapter 176. The pass through Trachis into Hellas [= Greece] is at its narrowest fifty feet wide. Yet it is not here but elsewhere that the way is narrowest, namely, in front of Thermopylae and behind it; at Alpeni, which lies behind, it is but the breadth of a cart-way. . . . To the west of Thermopylae rises a high mountain inaccessible and precipitous, a spur of Oeta; to the east of the road there is nought but marshes and sea. . . .

Chapter 177. These places, then, were thought by the Greeks to suit their purpose; for after due survey they reckoned that the foreigners could not make use of their multitude, nor of their horsemen; and therefore they resolved, that here they would encounter the invader of Hellas. . . .

Chapter 202. The Greeks that awaited the Persian in that place were these:—Of the Spartans, three hundred men-at-arms; a thousand Tegeans and Mantineans, half from each place; from Orchomenus in Arcadia a hundred and twenty, and a thousand from the rest of Arcadia; besides these Arcadians, four hundred from Corinth, two hundred from Phlius, and eighty Mycenaeans. These were they who had come from Peloponnesus: from Boeotia, seven hundred Thespians and four hundred Thebans.

Chapter 203. Besides these the whole power of the Opuntian Locrians and a thousand Phocians had been summoned, and came. The Greeks had of their own motion summoned these to their aid, telling them by their messengers that they themselves had come for an advance guard of the rest, that the coming of the remnant of the allies was to be looked for every day. . . .

Chapter 206. These, the men with Leonidas, were sent before the rest by the Spartans, that by the sight of them the rest of the allies might be moved to arm, and not like the others take the Persian part, as might well be if they learnt that the Spartans were delaying; and they purposed that later when they should have kept the feast of the Carnea, which was their present hindrance, they would leave a garrison at Sparta and march out with the whole of their force and with all speed. The rest of the allies had planned to do the same likewise; for an Olympic festival fell due at the same time as these doings; wherefore they sent their advance guard, not supposing that the war at Thermopylae would so speedily come to an issue.

Chapter 210. For the space of four days Xerxes waited, ever expecting that the Greeks would take to flight; but on the fifth, seeing them not withdrawing and deeming that their remaining there was but shamelessness and folly, he was angered, and sent the Medes and Cissians against them, bidding them take the Greeks alive and bring them into his presence. The Medes bore down upon the Greeks and charged them; many fell, but others attacked in turn; and though they suffered grievous defeat yet they were not driven off. But they made it plain to all and chiefly to the king himself that for all their number of human creatures there were few men among them. This battle lasted all the day.

Chapter 211. The Medes being so roughly handled, they were then withdrawn from the fight, and the Persians whom the king called Immortals attacked in their turn, led by Hydarnes. It was thought that they at least would make short and easy work of the Greeks; but when they joined battle, they fared neither better nor worse than the Median soldiery, fighting as they were in a narrow space and with shorter spears than the Greeks, where they could make no use of their numbers. But the Lacedaemonians fought memorably. They were skilled warriors against unskilled; and it was among their many feats of arms, that they would turn their backs and feign flight; seeing which, the foreigners would pursue after them with shouting and noise; but when the Lacedaemonians were like to be overtaken they turned upon the foreigners, and so rallying overthrew Persians innumerable;

wherein some few of the Spartans themselves were slain. So when the Persians, attacking by companies and in every other fashion, could yet gain no inch of the approach, they drew off out of the fight.

Chapter 212. During these onsets the king (it is said) thrice sprang up in fear for his army from the throne where he sat to view them. Such was then the fortune of the fight, and on the next day the foreigners had no better luck at the game. They joined battle, supposing that their enemies, being so few, were now disabled by wounds and could no longer withstand them. But the Greeks stood arrayed by battalions and nations, and each of these fought in its turn, save the Phocians, who were posted on the mountains to guard the path. So when the Persians found the Greeks in no way different from what the day before had shown them to be, they drew off from the fight.

Chapter 213. The king being at a loss how to deal with the present difficulty, Epialtes son of Eurydemus, a Malian, came to speak with him, thinking so to receive a great reward from Xerxes, and told him of the path leading over the mountain to Thermopylae; whereby he was the undoing of the Greeks who had been left there. . .

Chapter 219. . . . came deserters, while it was yet night, with news of the circuit made by the Persians; which was lastly brought also by the watchers running down from the heights when day was now dawning. Thereupon the Greeks held a council, and their opinions were divided, some advising that they should not leave their post, and some being contrariwise minded; and presently they parted asunder, these taking their departure and dispersing each to their own cities, and those resolving to remain where they were with Leonidas.

Chapter 220. It is said indeed that Leonidas himself sent them away, desiring in his care for them to save their lives, but deeming it unseemly for himself and the Spartans to desert that post which they had first come to defend. But to this opinion I the rather incline, that when Leonidas perceived the allies to be faint of heart and not willing to run all risks with him he bade them go their ways, departure being for himself not honourable; if he remained, he would leave a name of great renown, and the prosperity of Sparta would not be blotted out. For when the Spartans enquired of the oracle concerning this war at the very beginning, the Pythian priestess had prophesied to them that either Lacedaemon should be destroyed of the foreigners, or that its king should perish: which answer was given in these hexameter verses:

> Fated it is for you, ye dwellers in wide-wayed Sparta,
> Either your city must fall, that now is mighty and famous,
> Wasted by Persian men, or the border of fair Lacedaemon
> Mourn for a king that is dead, from Heracles' line descended.
> Yea, for the foe thou hast nor bulls nor lions can conquer;
> Mighty he cometh as Zeus, and shall not be stayed in his coming;
> One of the two will he take, and rend his quarry asunder. . .

Chapter 223. So the foreigners that were with Xerxes attacked; but the Greeks with Leonidas, knowing that they went to their death, advanced now much farther than before into the wider part of the strait. For ere now it was the wall of defence that they had guarded, and all the former days they had withdrawn themselves into the narrow way and fought there; but now they met their enemies outside the narrows, and many of the foreigners were there slain; for their captains came behind the companies with scourges and drove all the men forward with lashes. Many of them were thrust into the sea and there drowned, and more by far were trodden down bodily by each other, none regarding who it was that perished; for inasmuch as the Greeks knew that they must die by the hands of those who came round the mountain, they put forth the very utmost of their strength against the foreigners, in their recklessness and frenzy.

Chapter 224. By this time the spears of most of them were broken, and they were slaying the Persians with their swords. There in that travail fell Leonidas, fighting most gallantly, and with him other famous Spartans. . . .

The History of Herodotus, translated by G. Rawlinson (London, 1858–1860), book VII.

5

MEDIEVAL MUSLIMS AND CHRISTIANS, AND MODERN AGENDAS FOR THE MIDDLE EAST

In the modern era the years marked by the greatest tension and conflicts between Christians and Muslims, and between the West and the Middle and Near East, were undoubtedly, first, those following the end of the World War II, that led to the creation of the state of Israel and the crisis of European colonial empires, and, second, those following the Islamic extremists attack against two skyscrapers in New York and the Pentagon in 2001, and the United States invasion of Iraq in 2003. A corresponding period of great tension and conflicts between Christians and Muslims in the Middle Ages was that of the Muslim leader Saladin (d. 1193). It is therefore no coincidence that films on the Crusades, which were greatly influenced by modern issues, focus on Saladin's years and were made shortly after the two just-mentioned periods of the modern era.

Before examining the movies, it is necessary to present an overview of the main events concerning Muslims and Christians/Westerners during the era of Saladin (who was Sultan of Egypt and Syria), the history of the Middle East from the birth of the state of Israel to the late 1950s, and the conflicts characterizing the beginning of the third millennium.

Having created his own dominion, which included Egypt and Syria, by fighting against Muslim rivals, Saladin waited for the propitious moment to seize the Christian Kingdom of Jerusalem that had been created after the conquest of that city by European Christians in 1099. Despite defeating Saladin twice in the 1170s, the Christians began to weaken due to lack of strong leadership and disagreements among the nobles over the choice of a new ruler to replace the young King Baldwin IV who was seriously ill with leprosy and had no direct heir. In 1180, the marriage of his sister Sibylla, widowed two years earlier, to Guy of Lusignan, a French aristocrat who had arrived in the Holy Land a few years earlier, soured the spirits of the Christian nobility because one of the most powerful lords of the Holy Land, Raymond of Tripoli, wanted Sibylla to marry one of his supporters. In

DOI: 10.4324/9781003153139-6

1183, Baldwin IV gave the regency to Guy of Lusignan, took it away shortly after because of his military incompetence, and a few months before his death in May of 1185 assigned it to the expert Raymond of Tripoli.

Needing to strengthen their respective internal positions, Saladin and Raymond established a truce (the sultan had previously reached one with Baldwin IV between 1180 and 1182). The crisis in the Kingdom of Jerusalem erupted in the summer of 1186 when Baldwin V, a sickly 9-year-old boy from Sibylla's first marriage and whom Baldwin IV had appointed as his successor, died. Because she was Baldwin IV's closest relative, Sibylla was crowned queen by the patriarch of Jerusalem and crowned her husband, Guy of Lusignan, king. Raymond and Balian of Ibelin refused to submit to the new ruler. However, the insistent rumors about the connivance of Raymond with Saladin and the fact that he had let the Muslim troops that had defeated a Christian contingent pass through his lands induced Raymond to swear allegiance to Guy.

One of the new king's main supporters was Reynald of Châtillon, a French aristocrat who had come to the Holy Land in the 1150s. Having lost the Principality of Antioch and having spent fifteen years in a Muslim prison certainly sharpened his eagerness to regain a prestigious position and his desire for revenge against the faithful of Islam. The presence of an ineffective king in need of his support, as was Guy, was an ideal situation to achieve his aspirations. These goals, and his spirit of independence, had already emerged in the winter of 1182–1183 when he made an expedition to the Red Sea with ships whose components had been transported by camels. The Muslims were taken by surprise and Reynald's men managed to sink several enemy boats and sack some towns before being defeated and captured not far from Medina, one of the main Islamic holy places. The audacious raid created great embarrassment for Saladin and made Reynald the Muslims' most hated Christian leader. In the winter of 1186–1187 he gave the sultan another excuse to intervene against the Christians by attacking a Muslim caravan that passed near his lands. According to Islamic sources it was composed of pilgrims and merchants (one author adds that Saladin's sister was part of the group and that Reynald killed her), while Christian sources report that the caravan had an armed escort, which constituted a violation of the terms of the truce between Christians and Muslims.

Saladin entered the Kingdom of Jerusalem with a large army and Guy, convinced by Reynald of Châtillon and by the leader of the military order of the Templars, decided to face the Muslim army at the beginning of July 1187. Saladin preferred not to clash with his adversaries in open field, but rather to weaken them with frequent surprise assaults. In the meantime the lack of water, made unbearable by the intense heat, further weakened the Christians. Raymond of Tripoli and his men launched an attack against the Muslim lines and managed to escape (according to one source, they were let through thanks to an agreement made with Saladin). The remaining Christian forces retreated to two low hills, called the Horns of Hattin, and after a failed assault by their cavalry, Saladin's warriors advanced and won a clear victory.

In addition to inflicting numerous losses on their opponents, the Muslims captured many of them, among whom were Guy and Reynald. Saladin treated the former with courtesy and allowed him to be ransomed, but he had no mercy for the latter. He cut off his arm and then had his men execute him. To teach the Christians a lesson and weaken their morale, he also ordered the execution of the members of the military orders, the Templars and the Hospitallers, who represented the backbone of the Christian army. With the exception of Tyre, Saladin easily took over all the cities of the Kingdom. Jerusalem surrendered in the fall of 1187 after a brief siege. Unlike what happened in 1099 on the occasion of the Christian conquest of the Holy City, there were no massacres of civilians or looting. Having to reward his men, Saladin, however, granted freedom only to Christians who were able to pay their ransom. The sultan freed some of them using his personal funds, but the number of Christian prisoners for sale in that period was so high that the price of slaves dropped significantly.

In the meantime, news of what had happened in the Holy Land reached Europe and the pope proclaimed a crusade to recover Jerusalem. The first European ruler to respond to the call was the elderly German Emperor Frederick Barbarossa, whose expedition did not reach its destination because he died during the journey and most of his troops then returned home. The end of the conflict between the kings of England and France allowed them to take up the pope's call and concentrate on preparing for the Crusade. In the spring of 1191, the King of England, Richard Lionheart, and the King of France, Philip Augustus, arrived in the Holy Land, and thanks to them Acre was quickly retaken. To the pre-existing tensions between Richard and Philip were added those generated by the dispute for the title of king of Jerusalem. It was decided that it would remain to Guy of Lusignan who had in the meantime been freed by Saladin, and that at his death it would pass to the Italian nobleman Conrad of Montferrat, brother of the first husband of Sibylla. Until then, the royal income would be divided between the two. Conrad, who had been the first to rush to the aid of the Holy Land and who had ensured that Tyre did not fall, never accepted this agreement and often refused to cooperate with the English king. Philip returned to France in the summer of that year due to illness, while Richard remained in the Middle East until October 1192. He defeated Saladin in two battles, but although he made his way toward Jerusalem on a couple of occasions, he never got there and therefore failed to achieve his most important goal, the reconquest of the Holy City.

The clashes with the Muslims had all the same weakened his army, and Richard was also aware that even if he succeeded in taking Jerusalem, the majority of the crusaders would have considered their vow fulfilled and would have returned to Europe. Saladin could then have easily conquered the city again. Short of resources, exhausted by the war, and worried about the internal situation in their dominions, Richard and Saladin established a three-year truce in September 1192. The Christians retained most of their possessions on the coast and were allowed to make pilgrimages to Jerusalem. Richard, however, did not take advantage of this opportunity because he probably felt it was not honorable to visit the Holy City under those terms.

As in the late twelfth century, the Middle East was in turmoil in the years leading up to the 1963 release of the Egyptian film *Saladin the Victorious*. In May 1947, the United Kingdom declared that it could no longer handle the incandescent tension between the Muslim and Jewish populations of Palestine and turned the matter over to the United Nations. At the end of the year, the UN assembly approved a plan to establish the creation of the Jewish state of Israel and the Muslim state of Palestine, and granted Jerusalem the status of free city. Nonetheless, the armed conflicts between Muslims and Jews intensified and the latter attacked all the Muslim villages located in the territory assigned by the UN to Israel, causing numerous causalities and the flight of the majority of the inhabitants. On May 14, 1948, the state of Israel was officially proclaimed and was immediately recognized by the Soviet Union, the United States, and several other countries. The troops of the Arab League, which had always been against the creation of a Jewish state, attacked Israel the following day. Having emerged victorious from the conflict, the Israelis occupied most of the territories that according to the UN should have formed the state of Palestine. And again, many Muslims were forced to leave their homes and take refuge in what remained of the original state of Palestine and in neighboring countries.

Meanwhile in Egypt, the failure of the United Kingdom's promise to withdraw its troops from that country sharpened independence supporters' protests which were also directed against the king of Egypt who was blamed for subservience to Western powers. Among his opponents was the Committee of Free Officers which was very popular in the army and proposed to modernize Egypt and establish a somewhat Socialist and secular society. Under the leadership of Gamal Abdal Nasser (1918–1970), in 1952 they deposed the Egyptian ruler, forced the British to leave the country, and created a military dictatorship. Their aims clashed with those of the other main Egyptian independence movement, namely the Muslim Brothers, who wanted to create an Islamic state, and therefore opposed them strongly. From the moment he seized power, Nasser expressed the desire to lead a coalition of Muslim states to eliminate Israel and the Western presence in the Middle East. To achieve these goals and to strengthen Egypt economically, in 1955 the Egyptian statesman prohibited Israeli ships from using the Suez Canal which, by connecting the Mediterranean to the Red Sea, was a vital route for international trade, and in July 1956 he ordered its nationalization. In addition to Israel, these decisions greatly harmed the company, backed by French capital, that administered the Canal. In October of that year, France and the United Kingdom, eager to recover their recently lost positions, and Israel intervened militarily. British and French paratroopers took possession of the Suez Canal and with the support of English and French air power, the Israelis defeated the Egyptians and took possession of the Sinai Peninsula.

These actions deeply compromised the precarious balance of power in that area and did not reflect the changes that had occurred after World War II in the international arena then dominated by the opposition between the Soviet Union and the United States. Thanks also to Nasser's appeals, the Soviets threatened military actions against the aggressors if they did not withdraw. Concerned that the conflict could escalate, the United States condemned the aggression and submitted to the UN a petition for the immediate cessation of the occupations. In the face of such pressure, the United Kingdom, France, and Israel agreed to withdraw their troops. Although he was defeated militarily, Nasser turned out to be the winner in this affair. His prestige increased so much that in February 1958 he was able to achieve a major success in his pan-Arab project by uniting Egypt and Syria in the United Arab Republic.

The desire to establish a clear link between the history of the Middle East at the time of the Crusades and modern history can be seen at various points in the 1963 film *El Naser Salah el Dine* (*Saladin the Victorious*) by Egyptian director Youssef Gabriel Chahine (1926–2008), which recounts the most heroic and famous part of Saladin's life, namely the victory at Hattin, the conquest of Jerusalem, and the clashes with the Europeans who wanted to reconquer Jerusalem. It is not by chance that the film begins with an attack by warriors of the Kingdom of Jerusalem against a caravan of unarmed and peaceful Muslims, and with faithful of Islam who, having abandoned their homes because of the aggressions of the crusaders, took refuge with Saladin. Struck by their tragic condition and by the great violence of the Christians, the sultan decides to fight them. In reality, the conquest of Jerusalem and the surrounding territories by the Christians, between the end of the eleventh century and the beginning of the following century, induced few Muslims to flee, especially among the members of the wealthier classes. The new rulers did not impose a highly oppressive system on Muslims and many Muslim peasants in the Kingdom of Jerusalem were better off economically than their peers in the neighboring Islamic territories. As a result, most Muslims preferred to stay rather than face an uncertain future.

Those scenes in the movie are invented to emphasize that history was repeating itself. According to the director, the creation of the Kingdom of Jerusalem in the twelfth century had in fact produced upheavals in the Middle East similar to those that occurred following the establishment in 1948 of Israel (Nasser called Israel an instrument of European colonialism). As already mentioned, the birth of Israel provoked violent internal clashes between the Jewish population and the Islamic one, and wars between the new nation and the bordering countries led to flight, and sometimes the expulsion, of a great number of Muslim inhabitants from Israel and marked the beginning of the diaspora of the Palestinian refugees. The parallel was so obvious that for several years, in Middle Eastern movie theaters the spectators shouted 'Jews, Jews' every time the crusaders appeared in the film.

The creation of Israel also exacerbated the problem concerning Jerusalem—the third holy city of Islam—which according to the UN should have assumed the status of free city, but which the Israelis had largely occupied. The director did not fail to emphasize the Muslims' rights over it by having a lieutenant of Saladin say that 'Jerusalem has always been an Arab land.' The sultan himself later reiterated this notion by telling King Richard that it 'belongs to the Arabs.' Chahine, on the other hand, created a less explicit reference to the modern exploitation of the Arabs by Western powers by showing Muslim prisoners being forced to push the crusaders' siege machines under the scorching sun, a detail not reported in medieval sources.

For the modern Egyptians, Saladin's conquest of Jerusalem in 1187 echoed their 1952 revolution that put an end to the British presence in their country and the monarchy. In both cases the Westerners had been ousted and a legitimate indigenous government had been established. Even more obvious was the symbolism of the Third Crusade. Just as France and England had sought to reconquer Jerusalem in 1189–1192, the same European powers had attempted to regain control of the Suez Canal in 1956. The director also highlighted this connection visually, characterizing the components of the crusading army with different colors: blue for the English, red for the French, and white for the warriors of the Kingdom of Jerusalem. The arrangements of the Christian troops, in battle sequences, form stripes of different colors that recall the modern flags of France and the United Kingdom. In one scene, the juxtaposition of warriors in blue and white probably alluded to the flag of Israel, which had taken advantage of the Suez Crisis to occupy the Sinai Peninsula.

Except for the King of England, Richard Lionheart, a formidable but valiant enemy (an image similar to that found in medieval Muslim sources), all the crusader leaders are portrayed as warmongers, always ready to betray, and exclusively motivated by a desire for profit and conquest, just like the twentieth-century imperialist powers. The worst portrait is reserved for Reynald of Châtillon who, besides committing the already mentioned massacre of civilians, is portrayed as the person responsible for the breaking of the truce with Saladin and for the battle of Hattin. The fact that Reynald went against the will of the old king of Jerusalem is relevant in this regard. These are historical falsifications that the director used to underline that among the Westerners, both in the Middle Ages and in the contemporary age, the real power was in the hands of warmongers.

In the film the Europeans also are shown to have a strong contempt and hatred for the Arabs and are ready to act in all ways, including the most dishonorable ones, to harm them. In one scene, for example, in order to prevent an exchange of prisoners, the crusader leaders first eliminate the messenger bearing the news that Saladin accepted the proposal and then order the execution of Muslims with the excuse that the sultan had refused the offer. The arrival in the Christian camp of the crusaders freed by Saladin immediately after the heinous massacre effectively underlines the antithetical actions of the Westerners in comparison to the honorable ones of Saladin. The need to emphasize this led the director to distort what the medieval sources report about that episode. According to Muslim sources, King Richard put the Muslim prisoners to death so that they would not hinder the march of his troops, while Christian sources report that the English king carried out this action because the sultan had not delivered the ransom and the Christian prisoners on the agreed day.

The director stigmatized Westerners to emphasize the exemplary behavior of Saladin, whose representation echoed the figure of Nasser. When Saladin learns that King Richard is seriously ill, the sultan, with a great spirit of charity and courage, goes secretly to his adversary's tent to give him a medicine he prepared himself. Acting very humanely, he was also concerned about the conditions of the Christian prisoners. He visited them and suggested to one of them, a peasant from Normandy, to 'cultivate the fields instead of sowing sorrow.' Putting into practice the precept of the Koran to fight exclusively for the cause of God and not to attack first, Saladin uses weapons only in response to aggression and prefers to employ diplomacy rather than war. In the meeting with the crusader leaders who insolently tell him that if he wants peace he must accept their conditions, Saladin answers: 'Since when do aggressors impose conditions on the legitimate owners? You started this war; if you want peace truly, leave my country.' To the provocative question of whether that was a declaration of war, he replies that he hates war, but if necessary he would fight to defend his land.

When he goes to King Richard's tent to cure him, Saladin tries to convince his adversary to cease hostilities by pointing out the serious damage and suffering he has caused and at the end of the film the sultan suggests to the English king to tell the Europeans that 'war is not always the solution.' In this way the director also alluded to the fact that during the Suez crisis Nasser had been defeated militarily by France and England, but he had been victorious because, thanks to the use of diplomacy, he had managed to convince the Soviet Union and the United States to ask for the withdrawal of those nations' troops. The behavior and the words of Saladin finally made an impact on King Richard who, having gone to the sultan to ask for the end of hostilities, told him that fighting no longer made sense and that he had seen thousands of bodies of which he could not distinguish the crusaders from the Arabs. All were equal. Saladin generously imposed no conditions on the peace except that both rulers would promise never to use arms again.

The need to create a Saladin who was exactly the opposite of the crusader leaders led the director to omit some historical events and edit others. First of all, in the film there is no mention of the fact that Saladin ordered the execution of the members of the military orders captured in Hattin (the truthfulness of this episode cannot be doubted since the Muslim sources themselves mention it; see primary source A). Among the Christians who fell into the hands of Saladin's followers was Reynald of Châtillon. The director shows that Saladin kills Reynald but, unlike what is reported in the medieval Muslim texts in which the Christian is executed (see primary source B), in the film the sultan does not follow the suggestion of his advisors to put him to death and generously allows Reynald to face him in a duel with a sword (the crusader leader proves his evilness until the last moment by using an axe as well).

Chahine also shows that after the surrender of Jerusalem, the sultan grants freedom to all the inhabitants, neglecting the already mentioned circumstance that it was granted only to those who were able to buy it. Many Christians could not do it and were enslaved by the Muslims.

Referring to themes present in a famous speech by Nasser, the director highlights the hypocrisy of Europeans ready to mask their material interests with the Christian religion. Moreover, the Christianity of the Westerners did not follow the fundamental principles of that faith at all which are about peace. This particularity is also expressed visually. Except for King Richard's warriors, the cross, the symbol par excellence of that religion, is shown in various parts of the clothing and banners of the crusaders, and in the group scenes the great number of crosses overload the screen creating an oppressive effect. As a further indication of the profound religious manipulations carried out by the Europeans, the crosses are often turned ninety degrees to the right or left, thus appearing similar to swords.

The character who most embodies these distortions is Reynald of Châtillon's wife, referred to by the invented name of Virginia, probably a play on words by the director aimed at those who know Western languages (in Arabic such a juxtaposition does not work). Virginia is in fact the furthest thing from the virgin mother of Jesus. It is she who, after the death of her husband, instigates King Richard to organize a crusade against Saladin by telling him about the (false) atrocities committed by the Muslims in the Holy Land. Taking advantage of her attractiveness, she seduces all the 'bad' crusader leaders to gain power. Virginia's belligerent version of the Christian religion and her irreducible hatred towards Muslims are clearly expressed in the words she addresses to a Christian woman accused of having fallen in love with a Muslim.

> She no longer has the sacred hate in her heart! She gave her Christian body to an Arab, forgetting the war and that we will not win if we don't hate them.

On several occasions, Chahine also uses Saladin to condemn the un-Christian behavior of Westerners. For example, during a meeting with the crusader leaders Saladin states that both Christianity and Islam forbid bloodshed. In the aforementioned scene in which he suggests to a crusader to 'cultivate the fields instead of sowing sorrow', there is a reference to the Christian precept of turning swords into plows. To King Richard's remark that his conscience as a Christian would never find peace as long as the city of olives, i.e. Jerusalem, remained in Arab hands, Saladin replies that the sovereign would thus burn the branches of the olive trees. On other occasions, the sultan reprimands Richard for his obstinacy in wanting to fight, telling him that he was not doing it for Christianity but for his vanity and invites him to put an end to bloodshed, pointing out that this would have satisfied Allah (God in Arabic) and Christ.

Significantly, Chahine also entrusts the task of unveiling the contradictions of the Europeans' behavior and showing them what true Christianity is to an Eastern Christian, friend of Saladin and member of his army. His very name, Issa, Jesus in Arabic, already contains an extremely significant message. Jesus, that is the authentic Christian spirit, is not with the Europeans, but with Saladin. For example, addressing a Christian woman, Issa declares:

> You would rather follow those who turn their religion into a trade, to turn the holy places into markets in which to swindle the poor, pay for your blessings. The money goes into Europe's coffers, anyone who poses a threat to those profits faces fire, war, and death; blackmail in the name of the Holy Scriptures.

To the surprise of the woman who asks him why he fights his Christian brothers, he replies 'those who use the cross as an excuse to invade my land are not my brothers.' This concept is further emphasized when Issa tells her: 'I am a better Christian than you. I believe that taking what is not mine is an unforgivable sin; my belief in justice is the basis of my faith.' The outraged astonishment of the crusader leaders at seeing a Christian siding with the Muslims, their immediate conclusion that Issa can only be a mercenary, and the scornful derision of his response further underscore both their corrupt form of Christianity and their complete ignorance of the relationships that, according to the director, existed between the followers of Allah and those of Christ in the Middle East. Not surprisingly, it is Issa/Jesus himself who declares that Jerusalem has always been Arab and that the Arabs will prove that they can rule it in peace and respect for the other monotheistic religions. Chahine is so sensitive to this concept that he shows Saladin stopping the night attack against the crusaders when the ringing of the bells reminds him that it is Christmas Eve. He also wishes Issa 'Merry Christmas' (the scene is significantly accompanied by the sound of the call to prayer for Muslims gradually replaced by the Christian hymn 'Come Faithful') and invites King Richard and his men to celebrate that holy day for the Christians in Jerusalem. In an earlier scene, the sultan promises a Christian that he would soon be able to fulfill his wish to visit the holy city before going back to Europe.

Returning to Issa, Chahine does not merely point the finger at the errors of the Westerners and, like Jesus, Issa shows himself ready to teach what it means to be a true Christian through proper behavior. His story is intertwined with that of Louisa, a female warrior who serves in the crusader army. Issa's religiosity, his chivalrous behavior, and his love for her convince Louisa to change completely not only her attitude towards him, but also her way of being a Christian. At first Louisa is a fervent crusader and full of contempt for the Arabs. Captured by Issa while she was bathing, she is generously allowed to clothe herself. The woman not only does not keep her word not to flee, but wounds Issa, justifying her reprehensible action by saying that the promise made to an Arab is worthless. Having fallen into the hands of the Muslims, the crusader Amazon rejects Issa's offer of marriage with contempt, declaring that she would rather kill herself than marry an Arab. Thanks to the actions and words of Issa, who in the scene just recalled grants her freedom, Louisa questions her role as a warrior and decides to abandon her weapons and devote herself exclusively to the care of the wounded, among whom, on one occasion, is Issa himself. Her change is so profound that she bears with a composure worthy of a martyr the terrible insults of the crusaders and the death sentence for having helped a Muslim. Completely transformed, at the end of the film she accepts Issa's offer of marriage, who emphasizes that Louisa has to make that choice as a free woman and not as a prisoner.

The character of Issa also functions to show that at the time of Saladin the Arabs were not religiously divided and that the Eastern Christians sided with their Muslim brothers to face the aggressions of the crusaders. However, this does not match the reality. Generally speaking, in the Middle East during the Middle Ages the Muslims did not allow their Christian subjects to carry arms and only in a few cases of extreme necessity were they allowed to serve in the army, but never against Christian opponents. That spirit of collaboration and unity corresponded rather to the ideas that Nasser wanted to transmit to the Egyptian population, characterized by a large Christian minority. Worthy of note in this regard is the circumstance that in 1958, on the occasion of his speech for the union between Egypt and Syria, the Egyptian statesman recalled that in the Middle Ages Eastern Christians had sided with Muslims to face the aggression of the crusaders.

For Nasser unity in the Middle East also had to be achieved by overcoming ethnic and national divisions. As already noted, pan-Arabism was an important part of his political agenda and began to materialize in February 1958 with the proclamation of the union of Egypt and Syria in the United Arab Republic. The new state was short-lived. However, this did not diminish Nasser's popularity because his demise was attributed to his political adversaries and Western colonialists. References to an aspiration so relevant to Nasser could not be neglected in the film. Given that Saladin, before seizing the Kingdom of Jerusalem, had long fought to unify Egypt and Syria, the similarities between the past and the present are obvious. In *Saladin the Victorious*, the crusaders' opponents are in fact called Arabs, never Muslims or faithful of Islam. Saladin is given the title 'Sultan of the Arabs'; he calls himself 'servant of the Arabs' and often refers to Arabs as 'my people.' In addition, Chahine has him uttering a phrase that sums up Nasser's goal: 'my dream is to see the Arab nation united under one flag . . . hearts united and free of hate.' However, these ideas have no correspondence in historical reality. The real Saladin was Kurdish, and his warriors were largely Turks and Kurds. His unification of Egypt and Syria had come about through long and bloody wars waged against other Muslims. The conquest of Egypt had the appearance of a foreign invasion with religious implications. The Sunni Saladin had deposed the Shite dynasty of the Fatimids and consequently the Shite Muslims had been ousted from public administration. Saladin took possession of Syria by removing it from the heirs of his lord Nur Ad-Din on whose behalf he had taken Egypt.

Chahine also does not overlook the fact that Nasser presented himself as a secular political leader and opposed those who wanted to Islamize Egyptian society. The Saladin of the film therefore has similar characteristics to those of the contemporary Egyptian statesman and has nothing in common with the Saladin of the Middle Ages. Unlike in the late twelfth century, Islam in fact plays virtually no role in the film. Saladin is never referred to as a Muslim and a fighter for the Islamic faith. While calling himself a 'humble servant of God and the Arabs', he clearly favors the latter. The war against the crusaders is never called jihad, and the sultan states that both Islam and Christianity condemn bloodshed, but if necessary 'we will fight to defend our land.' Such an attitude by Saladin/Nasser reflected Chahine's approach to these issues. His family was Christian, and when asked about his religion, he replied that he was Egyptian.

As for Nasser's ideals of social equality, the film alludes to them by showing the simplicity and sobriety of Saladin's home, camp, and clothing. Saladin is presented, as are most of his men, wearing simple, often monochromatic clothes. This peculiarity is emphasized right from the beginning of the film where masses of Arabs dressed as peasants and armed with sticks run towards the camera while Saladin's face, who observes with approval, is superimposed on the scene. Historical truth is distorted here as well since Saladin's army consisted of professional soldiers, among whom were numerous warriors on horseback. With an ironic reversal of the Western stereotype of the exotic and extravagant Orient, Chahine contrasts the sobriety and simplicity of Saladin and his men with the colorful and rich clothing of the crusaders and their opulent and excessive camp equipped with acrobats, fire-eaters, and dancers, thus alluding to the profound difference between Nasser's Socialism and the consumer society of the Westerners.

Chahine also reveals the flaws of the Western world through the character of Virginia. Only members of a dysfunctional society could allow a woman to act in the sphere of politics and war and be stupidly manipulated by her. Significantly, her failure to behave as a woman is implicitly stigmatized by Saladin who refuses to address her as lady. The falsity and ephemerality of Western values are symbolized by Virginia's tragic end, who is disfigured by a siege tower falling on her. Without her beauty, her power over men vanishes, and one of the men she manipulated wonders if it was for that deformed being that he performed many evil deeds. Only after the disappearance of the ephemeral and false value of beauty does Virginia come to her senses and confess of having plotted to kill King Richard. However, she can no longer save herself from the infernal mechanism she has set in motion and therefore her accomplice strangles her.

Regarding the other female character, Louisa, in addition to what has already been noted earlier, the presence of a crusader amazon was probably intended to arouse disapproval toward the Western world and to remind the Muslim audience that there were women in the Israeli army (the colors of her clothing, blue and white, are similar to those of the Israeli flag). This peculiarity had already surprised the Muslim historians at the time of Saladin, who reported that among the Christian knights there were even some women. In such a world not even men were real men. In the film, beards and mustaches, symbols of masculinity in the Middle East, are, with the notable exception of the honorable enemy King Richard, the exclusive prerogative of the Arabs, including Issa. The scheming French king has some feminine features, while Reynald of Châtillon has an almost hysterical woman's tone and manners. With the devious Arthur, the director instead simply resorts to the equation that physical ugliness equals evil. In line with the idea that Western Christians were a society devoid of the most fundamental human values is the choice to depict (incorrectly) the king of Jerusalem as an old man whose wise advice not to fight Saladin is mocked by Reynald of Châtillon.

Primary sources

A) *Execution of the Templars and Hospitallers who had been captured at the battle of Hattin in 1187*

The Sultan [Saladin] sought out the Templars and Hospitallers who had been captured and said: 'I shall purify the land of these two impure races.' He assigned fifty dinar to every man who had taken one of them prisoner, and immediately the army brought forward at least a hundred of them. He ordered that they should be beheaded, choosing to have them dead rather than in prison. With him was a whole band of scholars and Sufis and a certain number of devout men and ascetics; each begged to be allowed to kill one of them, and drew his sword and rolled back his sleeve. Saladin, his face joyful, was sitting on his dais; the unbelievers showed black despair.

Arab Historians of the Crusades, selected and translated from the Arabic sources by F. Gabrieli. Translated from the Italian by E. J. Costello (Abingdon, 2010), p. 138.

B) *Saladin kills Reynald of Châtillon who had been captured at the battle of Hattin in 1187*

Saladin offered Reynald Islam but he refused. The sultan then drew his scimitar and struck him, severing his arm at his shoulder. Those present finished him off and God speedily sent his soul to Hell-fire.

The Rare and Excellent History of Saladin, or, al-Nawādir al-Sultaniyya wa'l-Mahasin al-Yusufiyya, by Bahā' al-Dīn ibn Shaddād, translated by D.S. Richards (Aldershot, 2001), p. 75.

6

MEDIEVAL CHRISTIANS AND MUSLIMS, AND WISHFUL THINKING DURING THE WAR IN IRAQ (2003–2005)

On September 11, 2001, two US airplanes were hijacked by Islamic militants into two skyscrapers in New York City known as the Twin Towers. Located in an area called the World Trade Center, both buildings caught fire and collapsed. Two other airplanes, which were to hit two other symbolic places of the United States, the Pentagon (the Ministry of Defense) and the White House (the residence of the President of the United States), did not reach their targets. There were about three thousand victims, mostly civilians who were in the offices of the Twin Towers and in the hijacked airplanes. The attack, claimed by the extremist Islamic organization Al-Qaeda, was a shocking episode for the United States which, for the first time in its history, suffered a foreign led attack within its borders.

Having obtained the approval of the UN and the support of NATO with the justification that it was a preventive defensive measure, the US government launched in October 2001 a military offensive against Afghanistan, a country ruled by the radical Islamic regime of the Taliban, where Al-Qaeda bases were located. The Taliban were quickly defeated and their regime brought down, but despite the US government's claim that the mission had been accomplished, the Taliban and Al-Qaeda continued to conduct attacks against the new Afghan government and Western troops from their bases in the mountainous region between Afghanistan and Pakistan. Building upon the victory over the Taliban government, and driven by the desire to provide further proof of American power in the hopes of making people forget the tragic episode of the Twin Towers, to punish a state that had not explicitly condemned the attack of September 11, 2001, to secure control of an area rich in oil, and to settle 'outstanding accounts' with the Gulf War of 1991, the US government turned its attention to Iraq, a nation ruled by Saddam Hussein. A massive media campaign was organized to prove that the Iraqi dictator, against whom the United States and its allies had intervened militarily a decade earlier for having invaded Kuwait, had helped Al-Qaeda and above all

DOI: 10.4324/9781003153139-7

possessed weapons of mass destruction that he intended to use against Israel and Western countries.

Unlike in the response to Afghanistan, this time the United States did not have the support of the other Western countries (the only exception was the United Kingdom) and of the UN that, after sending its inspectors in Iraq, declared that Saddam Hussein did not possess weapons of mass destruction and refused to approve the military intervention. The US government rejected this verdict and charged the UN with failing to search for those weapons properly. In the meantime, the US media pressure for a military intervention increased significantly, and those who opposed it were implicitly accused of lack of patriotism and betrayal. That pressure led the overwhelming majority of members in the US Congress to approve invading Iraq. Among the many Democrats in favor of the invasion was Senator Hillary Clinton, wife of former Democrat President Bill Clinton and future Democrat presidential candidate. In March 2003, US and British troops invaded Iraq, easily defeated the Iraqi army, and brought down the regime of Saddam Hussein, who was captured in December 2003 and executed in 2006. As happened in Afghanistan, despite the official declarations that the mission had been accomplished, peace in the country did not return. In fact, for several more years Saddam Hussein's supporters and Islamic radicals carried out guerrilla actions and attacks against the Iraqi government, the civilian population, and the American and British soldiers who were joined by military contingents from various countries who were tasked with trying to maintain order in the country.

In that period, the famous British director Ridley Scott made *Kingdom of Heaven* (2005). The film tells the story of Balian, a French blacksmith who learns that his father is Godfrey of Ibelin, a nobleman of the Kingdom of Jerusalem who went to France to ask forgiveness from him. Balian decides to follow him to the Holy Land and succeeds him after his death on the return journey. In the Middle East, Balian provides numerous proofs of his moral integrity and great courage. His greatest success is in inflicting so many losses on the Muslim army besieging Jerusalem that Saladin offers the Christians a generous agreement to surrender the city. Unlike *Saladin the Victorious*, Scott's film does not clearly project the contemporary situation into the past. Contemporary events did, however, exert a significant influence on the way *Kingdom of Heaven* was made. In fact, the director uses the film to show how one should act in order to achieve peaceful relations between Christians and Muslims, and to highlight what happens if hatred for the other, and religious fanaticism become ascendant. Scott's good intentions are undoubtedly praiseworthy, but they have produced a completely distorted past.

The distortion begins when, before the 'bad guys' came onto the scene, Scott presents the Middle East as an oasis of peace and mutual respect between Christians and Muslims. This oasis of good relations, Godfrey tells Balian, was being accomplished through the actions of Jerusalem's King Baldwin IV and Saladin. This point is later repeated to Balian by Tiberias, the palace master of Jerusalem's ruler: 'Saladin and the king united would create a better world.' In reality, there was truce, but no lasting peace. And Saladin was only biding his time. Following two heavy defeats, he decided to suspend hostilities while waiting for the death of the very ill king of Jerusalem to cause power struggles to break out among the kingdom's nobles, thus weakening the Christian front.

Through his thoughts and his deeds, Balian proves that he is moved by lofty ideals of tolerance and understanding for others, and possessed an exemplary religiosity which not only have no correspondence in the medieval world, but which are scarcely put into practice even in the contemporary world. Such ideas emerge from his first contact with the Muslims. During his journey to Jerusalem, he saw some of them intent on praying and, having learned from one of his companions who those people were and the meaning of their prayer, 'let us give thanks to God; it is good and just', the former blacksmith Balian then states that it 'resembles our prayer', thus emphasizing that between Christians and Muslims there are no real differences after all. The idea that the faithful of both religions worship the same divine entity who is called by different names seems to be implied. There is also a reference to the fact that no religion is superior to the others. Before the attack of Saladin's army on Jerusalem, Balian gives an impassioned speech to instill courage in the disheartened defenders of the city. Reminding them that they did not have to fight to defend the sacred places of Jerusalem, rather its inhabitants, he emphasizes that no one, neither Christians, nor Muslims, nor Jews, can claim special rights over Jerusalem because everyone has the same rights.

Balian's attitude towards God is completely unorthodox. Not only does he judge God's work, which should be inscrutable for men, but he is even ready to deny his existence if God is contrary to the actions considered rightful by Balian. During the siege of Jerusalem, in fact, he orders the bodies of the dead be burned to avoid an epidemic and to the patriarch's remarks that a burned body will not rise on the day of judgment, he replies that if they do not burn the corpses within three days everyone will die of an epidemic and God will understand what they have done and if he does not understand then it means that he is not God and they should not worry about him.

Balian is still a medieval knight and therefore could not be presented as a champion of non-violence. However, the director points out that he uses weapons only when he has to, that is, to defend himself from unjustified aggression and to protect the defenseless. It is no coincidence that at the end of the film he refuses to join King Richard's expedition to retake Jerusalem, even denying that he is Balian and pointing out that he is a blacksmith, obviously because that campaign was not intended to protect the people. If, instead, it is necessary to defend them, he does not back down and, after the defeat of the Christians at Hattin, he refuses Tiberias's invitation to go with him to Cyprus and sets out to protect the people of Jerusalem from Saladin's army. His first clash with a Muslim occurs only because the latter wants to take away his horse with the excuse that it was in his land. Balian is forced to kill him because the Muslim insists on fighting to the last blood. He does not, however, take the life of the Muslim's servant and even grants him freedom. On another occasion, even though he realizes that he is heading towards certain death, he and a small group of his men launch a charge against thousands of Muslim warriors to allow civilians to take refuge inside a castle.

This episode, one of the most spectacular of the film, not only never happened but, if compared to historical reality, it highlights the considerable distortions made by the director in the description of both the events and the motivations behind the actions of the Christian knights in the Holy Land (an element of considerable importance because it concerns the sphere of mentality). At that time, the assault of a small group of Christian knights against thousands of Islamic soldiers took place, but the motivations behind it were completely different from those shown in *Kingdom of Heaven*. Knowing that many Muslim warriors had entered the Kingdom of Jerusalem, in May of 1187 a small group of Templars and Hospitallers approached their opponents to discover their intentions. Given the large number of enemies, the commander of the Hospitallers suggested to retreat. The Templar leader told him that he cared a lot about his blond hair, thus implying that he was a coward. Not bearing the offense to his honor, the commander of the Hospitallers agreed to attack the Muslims. The obvious result of this suicidal charge, motivated only by warrior pride and rivalry between the Templars and the Hospitallers, was the death of almost all the Christians. Ironically, among the very few who survived was the Templar commander whose irresponsible behavior had caused those needless deaths.

Returning to Balian, the movie does not mention some details about the real Balian that would have cracked the perfect image of this character in the film. In *Kingdom of Heaven* he and Tiberias do not participate in the campaign that led to the battle of Hattin—Tiberias explicitly refuses to take part with his men. The 'good guys' could not in fact be present in an event produced by the fanaticism and unbridled hatred for Muslims of the 'bad Christians.' In reality, it was unthinkable that Balian of Ibelin and Raymond of Tripoli, who is the inspiration for Tiberias's character, could disobey the king's order to contribute to that campaign. If they had done so, they would have broken their oath of loyalty to the sovereign and would have lost their titles and possessions. The two nobles participated in the battle of Hattin and managed to save themselves from the Muslim encirclement probably thanks to an agreement with Saladin.

In the film, after some hard fighting to take Jerusalem, Saladin decides to talk to Balian. The latter tells him that his men will fight to the last and that for every Christian who died, ten Muslims would fall. He also promises 'to destroy every holy place, yours and ours, that leads man to madness', thus highlighting the little importance he attaches to religious symbols, i.e., the outward forms of religion.

According to a Muslim source, the real Balian instead threatened to kill every Christian in Jerusalem, including women and children, and their animals so that the Muslims would gain no economic advantage by taking over the city. He would also have exterminated the five thousand Muslims, who were in his hands, and destroyed all the Muslim holy places in Jerusalem. As can be seen, the actual threat was brutal, bloody, and contained no allusion to the consideration about 'places that make men mad.'

Nor is Balian the only 'positive' character with noble attitudes, high moral and religious principles, and respect for Muslims and appreciation for their culture and civilization that have no grounding in historical reality. A Hospitaller, who was part of Godfrey's retinue and guided Balian's first steps into the new world, expounds to the latter ideas about the Christian religion, and what it means to be a good Christian, that were unthinkable for a Christian in the Middle Ages, let alone for a member of a military order.

> I put no stock in religion. I've seen the lunacy of fanatics of every denomination be called the will of God. Holiness is in right action and courage on behalf of those who cannot defend themselves. . . . By what you decide to do every day you will be a good man . . . or not.

Sibylla, sister of Baldwin IV and queen at her brother's death, is often portrayed as a Muslim princess. She wears Middle Eastern clothes, has bodyguards and handmaidens with like clothing (this is also true for Balian when he is not fighting), likes temporary tattoos, and has both Christians and Muslims at her table whom she welcomes in Arabic. She also demonstrates knowledge of some of the fundamentals of Islam. When Baldwin IV meets Saladin, he gives him the most appropriate greeting in Arabic: 'Salam alaikum (peace be upon you).' Some words in that language are also spoken by Tiberias, another of the 'good guys.' In addition to ideas, in the film, clothing and language constitute a boundary line that separates the 'good guys' from the 'bad guys.' In fact, none of the latter wear Middle Eastern clothing or say a word in the language of the other, a visual and audio sign that they do not accept any form of intermingling with the Muslims. In reality, among all the characters mentioned in *Kingdom of Heaven*, probably the only one who spoke Arabic well was the super villain Reynald of Châtillon, not so much because he loved that language and the Muslim culture, but because he had spent many years as their prisoner.

The need to show that even among the faithful of Islam there were people endowed with high moral ideals and not marked by a fanatical hatred for the other led the director to distort the historical reality. In order to show how the leaders of the opposing camps, who tried to realize the 'Kingdom of Heaven', were very eager to solve with diplomacy the conflicts caused by the villains, Scott creates an episode that never happened. In the film, Saladin in fact enters the Kingdom of Jerusalem with his army to punish Reynald, guilty of having massacred the unarmed Muslims of a caravan. In spite of his serious illness and aware that traveling could have meant death for him, King Baldwin IV courageously leads his troops and stands between Saladin and Reynald's castle. However, the clash is avoided because diplomacy wins over war. Saladin had a conversation with the king of Jerusalem, and when the sovereign promises to punish Reynald, the sultan agrees to withdraw, thus avoiding a bloodbath. Saladin also proved to be very sensitive and worried about the health of his adversary. Noticing that Baldwin IV was suffering, the Muslim leader promises him that he will send him his doctors.

When Saladin seems to deviate from such perfect integrity, there is immediately someone who reminds him who the real Saladin is. Struck by the high number of losses inflicted by Balian on the Muslim army during the siege of Jerusalem, the sultan reproaches his lieutenant for having previously let Balian live (Balian in turn had in the past generously freed him). The officer replies that perhaps he should then have had a 'different master', thus reminding his lord how Saladin should behave. Also noteworthy is the answer the lieutenant gives Balian when after being captured by him, the Christian knight asks him what will become of him and his men. 'What you deserve. You reap what you sow. You've heard that before, right?' This phrase, a clear reference to a biblical precept, indicates how even the behavior of Saladin's good pupil was guided by moral principles like those of Balian. Returning to Saladin, the director does not fail to attribute to him ideas on the relationship between God and war that are exactly the opposite of the fanaticism of the 'bad' Christians for whom enemies can be defeated because 'God wills it.' To a Muslim religious leader who asked Saladin why he had withdrawn from Reynald's castle when the army of the king of Jerusalem had arrived, and pointing out that God alone determines the outcome of battles and on that occasion God was not with the Christians, the sultan in fact gave a very pragmatic explanation.

> The outcomes of battles are determined by God, but also by preparation, the number of soldiers, the absence of disease, the availability of water. You cannot maintain a siege with the enemy behind you.

In this regard, it should be noted that, like Chahine's Saladin, Scott's Saladin never refers to jihad and never incites his warriors by saying that God wants them to fight against Christians. In fact, the only Muslim to express such a concept is the just-mentioned Islamic cleric who is the Muslim version of the fanatical Templar commander. Unlike the latter, however, the Muslim does not participate in any armed clash.

In terms of his attitude towards religion and its symbols, Saladin's behavior is similar to that of Balian. To the latter's threat to destroy every place in Jerusalem sacred to Christians and Muslims, i.e., all those places that 'lead them to madness', Saladin replies, 'I wonder if it would not be better if you did that.' And to the Christian's subsequent question, 'How much is Jerusalem worth?', the Muslim replies: 'Nothing, Everything.' An exchange of opinions undoubtedly unthinkable in the Middle Ages (and, if one reflects a bit, for most people in our time as well). When Saladin occupied Jerusalem, he did not prove to be a fanatic and did not eradicate all references to Christianity in the city. Yet, it is an invention of the director that the sultan showed such great respect for the religion of his opponents that he put back in its place a cross that had been thrown to the ground.

In order not to show the ruthless and pragmatic side of the real Saladin, Scott does not go to the excesses of Chahine, who portrays a duel between the sultan and Reynald of Châtillon after Hattin, but, like his Egyptian colleague, avoids making any mention of the execution of members of the military orders who were captured in that battle. In truth there is a reference to that bloody episode, but it is understandable only by careful experts. Reynald of Châtillon's head is in fact shown on a pole above a pile of heads, among which we can recognize that of the Hospitaller who had been part of the entourage of Balian's father. Scott thus winks at the experts by telling them 'yes I didn't show that event, but I know it happened.'

Instead, the British director imitates Chahine by neglecting to mention that when Jerusalem surrendered, only Christians able to pay their own ransom were allowed to leave and that the others were made slaves of the Muslims (see primary sources A and B). Scott also idealizes Saladin's behavior by having Balian, surprised at Saladin's generosity, tell that after taking the city in 1099, the Christians had carried out a tremendous massacre. The sultan answers him that he was not those men, but he was Saladin, thus implying that his actions were guided by much nobler motives.

In the land of the Kingdom of Heaven, however, there are 'hawks' who oppose and sometimes destroy the work of the 'doves.' In addition to rejection and fanatical hatred for the other, the villains find justification for their disreputable behavior in a distorted and warmongering Christianity. 'God wills it' is their war cry as they prepare to fight the Muslims. To Tiberias's accusation that he plundered Muslims and his promise that he would soon make him pay for his misdeeds, Reynald sneers at him by replying with a phrase that is the exact opposite of the good guys' religious spirit. 'Oh and when shall this come to pass? Warn me when men are equal and the Kingdom of Heaven comes.' With even more sarcasm, Guy of Lusignan responds to Tiberias's remark, inspired by his concern for the consequences of the bad guys' actions and his desire to avoid conflict with Saladin—'I would rather live with men than kill them'—by stating: 'this sort of Christianity has its advantages, I suppose.' To the palace master's remark that he did not want war against the Muslims and that it was possible that the Christians might not win it, the head of the Templars—the armed wing of Reynald and Guy—retorts, pointing out that Tiberias's statement is blasphemous because 'an army of Christ bearing his holy cross cannot be defeated.' After which he exclaims: 'God wills it.' To Balian's observation that it was better that the Christian army did not leave Jerusalem to fight Saladin's troops in the open field, the Templar counters by saying that they had to go against 'the enemies of God.'

Moreover, the 'bad guys' are cowards and traitors. Not by chance, while the 'good guys' (Balian and Sibylla) make love, the 'bad guys' (Guy of Lusignan, Reynald of Châtillon and the Templars) make war. However, the latter do it in a dirty way by attacking unarmed civilians and taking intense pleasure in it. When Guy kills a Muslim and his blood splashes on the Christian's face, the camera zooms in on Guy's face expressing intense pleasure—a certainly unhealthy pleasure that is opposed to the healthy one of the 'good guys' intent precisely on making love not war.

From his first appearance, Guy is presented as a person animated by an implacable hatred for Muslims and Christians who wish to live peacefully with them. In fact, he reminds Balian that, after the death of Baldwin IV, 'there will be no place for friends of Muslims or traitors to Christendom like your father.' When he became king, Guy provided further proof of his ferocity and lack of respect for Muslims by plunging his knife into the throat of one of Saladin's ambassadors who had come to his court to seek justice for the misdeeds of Reynald of Châtillon, who had attacked a caravan of defenseless Muslims and killed Saladin's sister at the instigation of Guy, who was eager to have an excuse to fight the Muslims. 'Give me a war' are the significant words with which Guy urges Reynald to action (an allusion perhaps to the way in which the United States decided to invade Iraq in 2003).

Reynald is portrayed as the epitome of the villain/coward. The only Muslims he assaults and kills are unarmed civilians, among whom is Saladin's sister whom he insults by ripping off her veil before killing her. He is also so cowardly that after being saved from Saladin's punishment thanks to the intervention of Baldwin IV, he has no hesitation in submitting to the king, kissing his hand disfigured by leprosy. The evaluation expressed in the description of the actions of the 'good guys' is also valid for those of the 'bad guys.' Everything is invented and serves to delineate a clear division between what, according to the director, is right and wrong.

Just as he did for the 'good guys', Scott does not limit himself to the deeds of the 'bad guys', but highlights the ideas behind their behavior. When Balian, his father, and their companions are about to enter Messina to embark for the Holy Land, a preacher welcomes them by telling them twice: 'Killing an infidel is not murder, it is the path to Heaven.' Significantly, the director contrasts this belligerent form of Christianity with the part in which Godfrey explains to his son that the Kingdom of Jerusalem was on its way to becoming 'a better world than we have ever seen, a kingdom of righteousness, a kingdom of Heaven, there is peace between Christians and Muslims, we live together' and the scene in which Balian sees Muslims for the first time and comments on the similarity between Islamic and Christian prayers. Arrived in Jerusalem, Balian witnesses in a courtyard of the royal palace the execution of some Templars, guilty of having sacked a Muslim village, thus going against the truce established by the king, and comments that they died for having obeyed the orders of the pope.

Both this last remark and the statement of the preacher in Messina are inventions of the director that completely distort the historical reality. Saying this is not to claim that the motivations of every Western Christian who went to the Middle East in the Middle Ages to confront the Muslims were only religious, and that most of them did not hate the faithful of Islam and that their actions were not inspired by a form of belligerent Christianity that had nothing to do with the Christianity of the origins (a situation that also characterized other epochs, including the contemporary one, in which people fought in the name of God). However, it is inappropriate to use contemporary and secular ideas and sensibilities to judge actions and mentalities of the past. Therefore, it is necessary to remember that neither the pope nor his representatives had ever expressed those ideas. For the men of the Middle Ages, what we call Crusades were pilgrimages in arms whose objective was first to bring under the control of Christians the places where Christianity was born and, after taking them, protect them. By carrying out this mission, one could obtain forgiveness of one's sins and earn heaven.

The Templars and the members of the other military orders were warrior monks whose mission was to protect pilgrims and the Christian holy places from Muslims. The idea of a monk who also used weapons was not initially well received by the ecclesiastical hierarchies. This impasse was overcome by the intervention of one of the most prestigious churchmen and intellectuals of the twelfth century, Bernard of Clairvaux. A great supporter of the Templars, he wrote a treatise in which he clarified that if in the course of their duties, the Templars killed a Muslim, this action should not be considered a murder but a 'malicide', i.e. killing evil.

Undoubtedly for our contemporary sensibility such a way of thinking is unacceptable because it deprives the other of his humanity. It is however necessary to remember that in the twelfth century neither the pope nor churchmen ever declared that the objective of the Crusades and of the military orders was to eliminate the Muslims and that in this way paradise would be granted to them. The Templars certainly never backed down when asked to contribute to a campaign against the Muslims, but they never behaved like bandits thirsting for Muslim blood as Scott portrays them. And they never acted as assassins in the service of any lord of the Kingdom of Jerusalem (in the film Guy of Lusignan orders some Templars to assassinate Balian, who mocks them by asking if that was why they went to the Holy Land). Lastly, despite the image Scott creates of the Templars, it should be recalled that Reynald was not a member of that military order.

Nor does the way Scott portrays the patriarch of Jerusalem correspond to historical reality. He does not count him among the fanatical and warmongering Christians, but, with the clear intent of presenting all the ecclesiastical institutions of that time in a very bad light, he attributes to him attitudes and ideas that are extremely disreputable for an ecclesiastical leader. At the news of the approach of Saladin's army to Jerusalem, the patriarch in fact tells Balian that it is better to flee immediately. To the latter's question about what would have been the fate of the inhabitants if they had abandoned the city, the churchman replies that 'it is very unfortunate for the people but it is God's will', accompanying his words by making the sign of the cross. When Saladin asks to speak with Balian, the patriarch suggests to the latter to convert to Islam and then to repent later. The caustic irony of Balian's response clearly highlights his condemnation of the churchman's reprehensible behavior: 'You have taught me much about religion, your Eminence.'

By inserting other invented parts into the film, Scott shows that even some of the 'good guys' do not always behave with integrity. After Saladin's victory at Hattin, Tiberias turns to Balian and gives an unflattering summary of his actions, highlighting how lacking in ideals he now is.

> I have given Jerusalem my whole life. First, I thought we were fighting for God. Then I realized it was for riches and land. I was ashamed of it . . . God be with you. He is no longer with me.

In keeping with this attitude, Tiberias decides, unlike Balian, not to stay and defend the people of Jerusalem and to leave for safety in Cyprus. With the consent of Tiberias and Sibylla, King Baldwin IV suggests Balian marry his sister to prevent, after the death of the sovereign, Guy of Lusignan from becoming king and declaring war on Saladin. The hero of the film, however, refuses because this would imply the death of Guy and he cannot be responsible for it. The director insists on this point, contrasting Balian's idealism for which the Kingdom of Jerusalem 'is a kingdom of righteousness or nothing' with the pragmatism and Machiavellian overtones of Tiberias, who responds to Balian that 'Jerusalem does not need a perfect knight', and Sibylla who reproaches him by stating that 'a day will come when you will regret not having done a little evil for a greater good.' The director therefore shows that the hero of the film opposes the view that 'the end justifies the means' because 'the means change the end.'

In addition to the desire to present an upright hero with idealist and humanitarian values, and to describe how one should act in order to avoid conflicts between Christians and Muslims, one wonders if Scott's insistence on exalting an individual type of religiosity, which must be translated into correct behavior, and on denouncing the bad behavior of religious and secular institutions and the reference to the Machiavellian behavior of some of the 'good guys', are also the fruit of a reaction by the director to what happened in March 2003. On that occasion, it was not only the American Republicans—inclined to an aggressive foreign policy and proponents of a warlike version of Christianity that had nothing Christian about it (it should be remembered that the American president George W. Bush always presented himself as a fervent Christian and his supporters had the same characteristic)—who voted in favor of the invasion of Iraq. Giving in to the enormous media pressure and in order not to lose the favor of the majority of their voters, so did most of those who in theory should have defended humanitarian values and declared themselves against the unjustified use of force (the Democrats in the United States and the Labourists in the United Kingdom). Like Balian in *Kingdom of Heaven*, righteous and well-meaning individuals at the beginning of the third millennium could therefore only rely on themselves and hope that their upright behavior would save someone and serve as an example to those who shared their ideas. Since we cannot know the director's mental processes, this is obviously only an indemonstrable hypothesis. The fact that he was influenced by what was going on while making the film, however, is proven by the following caption placed at the end of the film: 'About a thousand years later peace in the Kingdom of Heaven is still elusive.'

Although Scott points out that a peaceful coexistence between Christians and Muslims would be possible if everyone behaved like the 'good guys' in his film, he reveals that he has some unconscious stereotypes about Muslims in the Middle East. In fact, on a couple of occasions he projects into the Middle Ages the contemporary Western technological superiority that has only been acquired since the Industrial Revolution in England in the eighteenth century. Arriving in the land left to him by his father, Balian, a blacksmith who had always lived in

France until then, teaches the natives how to find water and create an irrigation system for the fields. In the film it is clearly seen that Balian and his men prepare the irrigation tool called water wheel, a technique known in the Mediterranean area in classical Antiquity and that the Europeans, after having 'forgotten' it due to the upheavals following the end of the Roman Empire, re-learned when they conquered the lands occupied by the Muslims in southern Europe. In the Middle Ages, through the knowledge learned from the texts and experiences of classical Antiquity, it was therefore the Muslims who were scientifically and technologically superior to the Europeans. In a scene from the siege of Jerusalem, the Westerner Balian proves to be technologically more advanced than his Muslim adversaries, a fact that allows him to nullify the superiority of Saladin's army. Throwing some harpoons, connected to counterweights, against the siege towers of the Muslims that were near the walls of Jerusalem, Balian succeeds in making them fall, thus preventing Saladin's warriors from entering the city. The message seems to be 'You Easterners may have a large number of sophisticated weapons; however, we Westerners are superior and always devise a way to easily nullify your superiority of armaments.'

Primary sources

A) *Treaty for the surrender of Jerusalem in 1187*

The basic provision in the treaty was that they would pay ransoms, for every man ten Tyrian dinars, for every woman five dinars and for every child, male or female, a dinar. All who produced the ransom would secure their freedom, otherwise they would be made captive.

The Rare and Excellent History of Saladin, p. 78.

B) *Fate of the Christians who could not pay their ransom after the surrender of Jerusalem in 1187*

About 15,000 were unable to pay the tax, and slavery was their lot; there were about 7,000 men who had to accustom themselves to an unaccustomed humiliation, and whom slavery split up and dispersed as their buyers scattered through the hills and valleys. Women and children together came to 8,000 and were quickly divided up among us, bringing a smile to Muslim faces at their lamentations. How many well-guarded women were profaned, how many queens were ruled, and nubile girls married, and noble women given away, and miserly women forced to yield themselves, and women who had been kept hidden stripped of their modesty, and serious women made ridiculous, and women kept in private now set in public, and free women occupied, and precious ones used for hard work and pretty things put to the test, and virgins dishonoured and proud women deflowered, and lovely women's red lips kissed and dark women prostrated, and untamed ones tamed, and happy ones made to weep! How many noblemen took them as concubines, how many ardent men blazed for one of them, and celibates were satisfied by them, and thirsty men sated by them, and turbulent men able to give vent to their passion. How many lovely women were the exclusive property of one man, how many great ladies were sold at low prices, and close ones set at a distance, and lofty ones abase, and savage ones captured, and those accustomed to thrones dragged down!

Arab Historians of the Crusades, pp. 162–63.

7

THE BLACK DEATH, EXISTENTIALISM, OLD AND NEW FEARS, AND PRIVATE MATTERS

The Seventh Seal (1957) by Swedish director Ingmar Bergman (1918–2007) is considered by critics to be the best film about the Middle Ages, and some scenes have become part of popular culture. The plot is quite simple. Swedish knight Antonius Block and his squire Jöns return home after being on the Crusades for many years. On a beach Antonius meets Death but manages to block her by convincing her to play chess with him. The agreement is that during the game, Death will let the knight live and if Antonius wins, he will be spared. Afterwards, the knight explains that he has decided to obtain some time to perform a meritorious action that would give meaning to his life.

The two men's return is marked by rumors of ominous signs and gruesome events. Two horses devoured each other, in a cemetery the graves opened and the remains of the dead were scattered everywhere, and at sunset four suns appeared. Some rumors involve the plague that is claiming victims in the surrounding areas. The two men see some of the effects of the disease: a few deaths and some abandoned houses. Outside a church they come across a chained girl who, accused of being a witch, of having had carnal relations with the devil, and of being the cause of the plague, has been condemned to be burned at the stake at dawn. Shortly after, a lugubrious procession of penitents, who ask God for forgiveness by whipping themselves, arrives at an inn, interrupting the cheerful atmosphere created by the performance of a small company of wandering actors composed of Skat, Jof, and the latter's wife, Mia. The knight makes the acquaintance of the latter two and their child, Mikael, whom he invites to join him and his squire to cross together a forest beyond which there is his castle; the group is later joined by a blacksmith named Plog whose wife had run away with Skat.

During the journey, the knight and the squire witness the burning of the 'witch' and shortly before reaching the castle, Antonius distracts Death thus saving the family of actors. Having then accomplished a significant act in his life, the knight is

DOI: 10.4324/9781003153139-8

ready to face his fate. Shortly after his arrival at his castle from which everyone has fled except his wife Karin, Antonius and his companions are taken away by Death. This occurs while Karin recites the passage from the Apocalypse of John where the opening of the seven seals of the text is mentioned, showing the various stages leading up to the Final Judgement. The film ends with Mia and Jof waking up against the backdrop of a sunny day. The man claims to glimpse Death in the distance, who is taking away those who were in the castle, but Mia sees nothing and so the two of them and their baby leave towards the sun of the new day.

The historical setting in which the film takes place is accurate. In the middle of the fourteenth century, the plague hit Sweden, claiming many victims. Several important scenes of the film mirrored art and literature of the late Middle Ages; more precisely, the director sometimes anticipates themes in works of the fifteenth century, presenting them in the year 1350. For example, the suspension that Block gets from Death is inspired by that obtained in the late medieval play *Everyman* by the main character to end the play. The images of the chess game between Death and Antonius, Death sawing a tree where a man has taken refuge, and the Dance of Death are all taken from fifteenth-century frescoes. In his autobiography, the director claims to have seen them as a child in a church where his father, a Protestant pastor, went to preach, but this observation seems to be one of his stratagems to give a touch of naturalness to his sources of inspiration and thus divert viewers and critics from the modern intellectual background of the film. With the same intent, he emphasizes the similarities of the experiences and problems of men in the Middle Ages and the modern age.

> In my film the crusader returns from the Crusades as the soldier returns from war today. In the Middle Ages, men lived in terror of the plague. Today they live in fear of the atomic bomb. *The Seventh Seal* is an allegory with a theme that is quite simple: man, his eternal search for God, with death as his only certainty.

The reference to the similarities between the knight returning from the Crusade and modern veterans is in fact a consideration that does not hold up because in *The Seventh Seal* Antonius never mentions the disgust for what he did during that 'holy war.' Rather, he explains his existential malaise in terms of having devoted himself to futile activities without ever having accomplished anything significant: 'My life has been a futile pursuit, a wandering, a great deal of talk without meaning.' The fact that among these futile actions was having gone to the Holy Land is therefore only implied.

The allegory of the fear of the plague as the fear of the nuclear holocaust that characterized the world in the 1950s similarly comes up short. Perhaps, for those who did not live in that period, it is difficult to understand fully the atmosphere created when it became known that both the United States and the Soviet Union had nuclear weapons capable of destroying all of humankind. For example, during the last twenty-five years of the Cold War, when I was born and grew up, except for a few isolated Cassandras, that terror never existed because it was clear that the two superpowers were more or less equal in the field of nuclear weapons and knew that, if they used them, there would be neither winners nor losers.

From what can be deduced from studies of the years in which the film was released, in that period fear was more widespread in some countries, especially in the United States (it became more intense during the crisis that broke out because of the presence of Soviet atomic bombs in Cuba in 1962), but it does not seem that it had, for example, marked Sweden too much. Moreover, to relate the terror of the plague in the Middle Ages to the fear of the atomic bomb does not hold much water. Unlike the rather remote possibility of a nuclear holocaust, the plague in the middle of the fourteenth century was not a looming fear, but a tragic reality that in some parts of Europe killed more than half of the population.

The reference to the inevitability of death seems more appropriate, but it is not the only theme of the film. In fact, Bergman inserted into a plausible medieval setting a mixture of reflections on the existence of God and the role of men in earthly life. These reflections were influenced both by his long and difficult detachment from the education imparted to him by his father, a Protestant pastor, and by the themes characteristic of existentialism which were very much in vogue among many young people and intellectuals of the Left at the end of the 1940s and in the 1950s—a fundamental period for Bergman's intellectual formation. With regard to existentialism, it is necessary to take into account the influence on *The Seventh Seal* of the ideas of the least dogmatic exponent of that current of thought, Albert Camus (1913–1960). Of particular importance is the fact that in 1947 this French intellectual published a novel of great success, *The Plague*, a work that right from its title highlights the connection with *The Seventh Seal*.

Set in the 1940s, in the Algerian city of Oran (then under French rule), Camus's novel describes the various reactions of the inhabitants when the plague spreads through the city, sealed off by the central French authorities to prevent the spread of the epidemic. Notably, the behavior of Father Paneloux who, believing the plague to be a divine punishment for the sins of the citizens of Oran, delivers a fiery sermon on the sins of men and the just punishment of God is contrasted by that of Dr. Rieux, the narrator of the book. In addition to doing his best with other volunteers to bring relief to the sick, Rieux works to find a cure for the disease. Though most of the protagonists die, the story ends positively because Rieux creates a vaccine and the plague ends and life returns to the way it was. Although the doctor warns his fellow citizens and the authorities that the epidemic could return, he claims to have written the account of what happened because 'in the midst of scourges one learns that in men there are more things to admire than to despise.'

The nucleus of Camus's thought is constituted by the recognition of the absurdity of the human condition, which must not be translated into a passive acceptance. Contrary to pessimism and nihilism, he supported the necessity of healing from such situations through solidarity among human beings. Essential to achieve healing is the awareness of the absurdity of existence. The different phases of this process were expressed in *The Plague*, which represents the culmination of the evolution of Camus's thinking.

The movie *The Seventh Seal* follows a similar path, with the result that its characters express ideas that have little or nothing to do with the Middle Ages during which religion and God had a fundamental role. On this point it must be admitted that our knowledge about this era is largely based on the writings of churchmen or extremely devout laymen and therefore one should not make hasty generalizations about the medieval mentality. Even so, strong doubts about the existence of God or even nihilism are anachronistic for the Middle Ages.

Several dialogues in *The Seventh Seal* express well what ideas Bergman was referring to.

Entering a church, the knight decides to confess without realizing that in the confessional there is not a priest but Death.

KNIGHT: I want knowledge.

DEATH: You want guarantees?

KNIGHT: Call it whatever you like. Is it so cruelly inconceivable to grasp God with the senses? Why should He hide himself in a mist of half-spoken promises and unseen miracles?

Death doesn't answer.

KNIGHT: How can we have faith in those who believe when we can't have faith in ourselves? What is going to happen to those of us who want to believe but aren't able to? And what is to become of those who neither want to nor are capable of believing?

The knight stops and waits for a reply, but no one speaks or answers him. There is complete silence.

KNIGHT: Why can't I kill God within me? Why does He live on in this painful and humiliating way even though I curse Him and want to tear Him out of my heart? Why, in spite of everything, is He a baffling reality that I can't shake off? . . .

KNIGHT: I want knowledge, not faith, not suppositions, but knowledge. I want God to stretch out his hand toward me, reveal Himself and speak to me.

DEATH: But He remains silent.

KNIGHT: I call out to Him in the dark but no one seems to be there.

DEATH: Perhaps no one is there.

KNIGHT: Then life is an outrageous horror. No one can live in the face of death, knowing that all is nothingness.

DEATH: Most people never reflect about either death or the futility of life.

KNIGHT: But one day they will have to stand at that last moment of life and look toward the darkness. . . .

KNIGHT: In our fear, we make an image, and that image we call God.

In his desperate search for an answer to his questions Block also turns to Tyan, the girl who is about to be burned because she is accused of being a witch. During the execution of the young girl, the knight and his squire exchange anguished remarks on the afterlife, the impotence of men, and the absurdity of existence. Something similar occurs in the dialogue between Block and Jöns at the end of the film when Death is about to take everyone in the castle.

Another scene, the procession of the Flagellants, is plausible, considering the reactions that a tragedy like the plague can trigger and to what mortifications an exasperated desire for expiation can lead. However, the fiery sermon delivered by the churchman who leads these penitents does not fully correspond to medieval sermons. The references to the plague as divine punishment and to the fact that one can die at any moment are in fact accurate, but the way in which the churchman addresses very specific individuals has no correspondence with what we know about the Middle Ages.

Bergman claimed here to have been inspired by a sermon by the aforementioned character from *The Plague*, Father Paneloux, but, except for a generic similarity regarding the detail that the disease is a divine punishment that men have deserved for their sins (a common theme in this type of sermon), the two texts are completely different. The director's observation must therefore be classified as an attempt to place himself in line with Camus's thought.

Returning to the film, we note that Jöns's harsh criticism of the churchman's sermon is also anachronistic.

> This damned ranting about doom. Is that food for the minds of modern people? Do they really expect us to take them seriously?

Such a comment corresponds to the thoughts of a twentieth-century person about a religious practice of the Middle Ages. It is noteworthy that Jöns defines himself and those who think like him as 'modern people.' The same consideration applies to the dialogue between Jöns and the painter intent on portraying the Dance of Death in a church.

Jöns represents a sort of counterbalance to Antonius Block, who painfully tries to find an answer to his doubts about God. The squire has no doubts at all. There is nothing after this life, and if God exists, it is an obscure and indefinable entity that is completely uninterested in humans. The only things the squire believes in are what he sees and touches. His aspirations concern the satisfaction of the senses. The exchange he has with the knight after his remark about 'modern people' clearly indicates his thoughts on such matters.

JÖNS: Allow me to point out that I've either read, heard or experienced most of the tales which we people tell each other. . . .

JÖNS: Even the ghost stories about God the Father, the angels, Jesus Christ and the Holy Ghost—all these I've accepted without too much emotion. . . .

JÖNS: My little stomach is my world, my head is my eternity, and my hands, two wonderful suns. My legs are time's damned pendulums, and my dirty feet are two splendid starting points for my philosophy. Everything is worth precisely as much as a belch, the only difference being that a belch is more satisfying.

With remarkable irreverence, Jöns describes his experience at the Crusade.

> For ten years we sat in the Holy Land and let snakes bite us, flies sting us, wild animals eat us, heathens butcher us, the wine poison us, the women give us lice, the lice devour us, the fevers rot us, all for the Glory of God. Our crusade was such madness that only a real idealist could have thought it up.

He further illustrates his thoughts on the Crusade later when he meets Raval, the clergyman who convinced the knight ten years earlier to travel to the Holy Land and who became a thief stealing from the dead and threatening the defenseless.

> When I see you, I suddenly understand the meaning of these ten years, which previously seemed to me such a waste. Our life was too good and we were too satisfied with ourselves. The Lord wanted to punish us for our complacency. That is why He sent you to spew out your holy venom and poison the knight.

Even at the beginning of the film, Jöns reveals similar ideas, singing a refrain that with his usual desecrating spirit emphasizes the distance of God from earthly life where instead his 'crony' the devil dominates.

Probably with the same intent, in the screenplay Bergman included the following ditty about blind, bastard fate that Jöns sings after finding a dead man on the road: 'One moment you're bright and lively, / The next you're crawling with worms./Fate is a terrible villain / And you, my friend, its poor victim.'

Again through a ditty early in the film, the squire emphasizes that carnal pleasure is what he is all about:

> Squeezed twixt the thighs / On a bed of sighs. / That's the only way to be / For a man like me (in this case, too, the screenplay is more 'scandalous': 'Between a strumpet's legs to lie / Is the life for which I sigh.')

In a later scene, after a painter, intent on painting the Dance of Death, has described to him the effects of the plague, the squire first states: 'No matter which way you turn, you have your rump behind you. That's the truth.'

The painter reinforces that reflection by stating: 'The rump behind you, the rump behind you, there's a profound truth.'

The squire then draws a picture and thus summarizes the Jöns-thought.

> This is squire Jöns. He grins at Death, mocks the Lord, laughs at himself and leers at the girls. His world is a Jöns-world, believable only to himself, ridiculous to all including himself, meaningless to Heaven and of no interest to Hell.

In the Middle Ages there were some writers who, taking up the themes of classical Antiquity, stressed that man's destiny was in the hands of fate, which conditioned success and misfortune. In contrast to the idealizing themes very much in vogue in the thirteenth and fourteenth centuries, other authors also praised the satisfaction of the senses and the desire to live fully what the earthly life offered, stressing the need to take advantage of every opportunity because the moment is fleeting and there is no certainty of tomorrow. For example, the Italian poet Cecco Angiolieri (c. 1260–c. 1312) wrote:

> If I were fire, the world I would burn; / if I were wind, I would blow it away; / if I were water, I would make it drown; / if I were God, I'd send it deep below. / If I were Pope, I would be happy, too, because all Christians I would torment; / if I were Emperor, you know what I would do? / I would cut off everybody's head, all round. / If I were Death, after my father I would go; / if I were Life, away from him I'd flee; / and I'd act the same way to my mother. / If I were Cecco, as I am and was, / I'd take the young and pretty women; / the old and ugly I would leave to others.

In a famous sonnet, the Florentine banker, statesman, and poet Lorenzo De' Medici (1449–1492) states: 'Oh how beautiful is youth / Which escapes nonetheless / Let who wants to be happy be / As there is no certainty of tomorrow.'

There are also several examples of medieval authors who criticized and satirized the customs of churchmen. None, however, placed all those considerations alongside an explicit denial of God and the afterlife as Jöns does. The same conclusion applies to his description of his world and philosophy (one cannot, of course, comment on what people of that period thought but did not put in writing). To my knowledge there has been no study on the sources used by Bergman. Probably he was inspired by goliardic and satirical texts of the modern era.

A mixture of themes characteristic of the Middle Ages and observations influenced by modernity can be detected in the dialogues between the patrons present in an inn as they discuss the news and rumors about nearby areas. For example, the fact that the spread of the plague was foretold by ominous signs corresponds to what was reported by medieval sources.

Though medieval preachers did not fail to include lust among the sins that men and women had to pay for with the plague, it is a fantasy of the director what a woman reports on that subject.

WOMAN: But there have been other things too, such things that can't even be spoken of. (Whispers) Things that mustn't be named—but the priests say that the woman carries it between her legs and that's why she must cleanse herself.

OLD MAN: Judgment day. And the Riders of the Apocalypse stand at the bend in the village road. I imagine they'll come on judgment night, at sundown.

WOMAN: There are many who have purged themselves with fire and died from it, but the priests say that it's better to die pure than to live for hell.

These considerations are in fact the result of the modern perception of the Middle Ages, according to which in those centuries people were so obsessed with sex and sin that they reached extreme forms of expiation. The same conclusions apply to the connection—woman, witch, sex, devil, plague—present in the film. In the Middle Ages many women were burned at the stake because they were accused of being witches who had carnal relations with the devil (though their number was much higher during the early modern period), but they were not used as scapegoats during the plague of the fourteenth century. Instead, it was the Jews who were blamed for the epidemic.

The film is not only characterized by the observation of the absurdity of existence and the materialistic considerations of the squire. In line with the principles enunciated by Camus in *The Plague*, the only salvation from the absurdity of the human condition and the only way to define oneself as a real human being can be obtained through solidarity, which must emerge especially in the most dramatic moments. And in fact, the super materialistic Jöns is the one who proves such quality. He saves an orphaned girl from the perfidious Raval. Moreover, after making some advances to the girl without too much conviction (he says that he could have taken her by force but he underlines that such relationship is not for him because 'it runs a little dry in the end'), Jöns takes her with him showing her a great affection. Subsequently the squire saves Jof from Raval's clutches, intent on venting his wickedness on the actor. The good Jöns would have also wanted to save Tyan from the stake, killing the soldiers in charge of burning her, but he realizes that it would have been of little use since the girl was already half dead. Antonius, however, defies the flames to give her water and a sedative for the pain.

The most significant act of solidarity in the film, however, is that of the knight who gives meaning to his life by distracting Death at the moment when it was about to take possession of Mia, Jof, and their child. It is noteworthy that they are the only ones to save themselves from Death (a highly improbable event since they came into contact with people who will die of the plague).

Many years after that film, Bergman tried to make deep sense of his film and thus hide the references he made in the film to the problems and aspirations that had characterized his sentimental and professional life. In his book *Images: My Life in Film* (1990) he states:

> I infused the characters of Jof and Mia with something that was very important to me: the concept of the holiness of the human being. If you peel off the layers of various theologies, the holy always remains.
>
> I also added a playful friendliness to the family picture. The child brings about the miracle, and the juggler's eighth ball stands still in the air for one breathtaking moment, a microsecond.

It seems quite clear that Bergman used some of the characters and scenes in the film to represent personal problems and aspirations, including his problematic marital experiences. These were complicated by his difficulty in reconciling the roles of husband, father, and not-yet-established showman, and by his emotional mutability. When *The Seventh Seal* was released, Bergman was in his third marriage (which was already over and officially ended shortly thereafter) and had six children, and had in the meantime had several extramarital affairs; the director gives a brief but significant description of all this in his autobiography. In the dialogue between Plog and Jöns, the everyday problems of married life that had distressed Bergman are emphasized.

JÖNS: Yes, it's hell—with women and hell—without them. So, however you look at it, it's still best to kill them off while it's most amusing.

PLOG: Women's nagging, the shrieking of children and wet diapers, sharp nails and sharp words, blows and pokes, and the devil's aunt for a mother-in-law. And then, when one wants to sleep after a long day, there's a new song—tears, whining and moans loud enough to wake the dead.

In his autobiography, Bergman recounts the situation he found himself in during his second marriage in this way.

My family had expanded. In the spring of 1948, the twins were born and we moved into a five-room apartment in a new area outside Gothenburg. I also had a Spartan little room right at the top of the theatre and spent the evenings there editing scripts, writing plays and films. Ellen's stepfather killed himself, leaving large debts. My mother-in-law and her small son moved in with us. They settled in my study next to Ellen's and my bedroom. Newly widowed, Ellen's mother often cried at night and, in addition to that, Lena, my elder daughter, lived with us because Else was still ailing. The family was completed by a kindly but gloomy person who was to help in the household. We were ten people in all. Ellen had so much to do; she could only occasionally devote time to her profession. Marital complications became more and more infected by all this. Our sex life, which had been our deliverance, ceased because of the proximity of my mother-in-law and her little son through the thin wall. I was thirty and had been kicked out of Svensk Filmindustri after the fiasco of *Crisis*.

My domestic finances were stretched. Added to our other troubles were bitter quarrels about money . . . Home seethed with crying children, damp washing, weeping women and raging scenes of jealousy, often perfectly justified.

It is therefore no coincidence that the knight saves a family of wandering actors from death. The beautiful, sweet and understanding Mia, who even though she does not understand anything of the knight's anguish, knows how to infuse him with moments of peace and serenity through a simple gesture such as offering him milk and strawberries, thus making him understand the absurdity of his existential malaise. With good-natured patience, she puts up with the eccentricities of her imaginative actor husband to whom appear things that she does not see, and in spite of this, she still tells him that she loves him. Mia therefore represents both the distributor of human solidarity Camus style and the ideal wife that Bergman would have liked to have had.

Confirming what the director put of himself in the film is the fact that in those years Bergman had a long relationship with the actress, Bibi Andersson, who plays Mia (the screenplay is dedicated to her). It is therefore obvious that in *The Seventh Seal* the sentimental and professional relationship between Mia and Jof mirrors the one in real life between the actress and the director.

It should also be noted that Jöns saves Jof, an actor full of fantasies but nice and honest, in short, a good man. It is clear that Bergman identifies with him and it is not by chance that he 'kills' the other actor, the vain, false, and lying Skat who, apart from his good looks and his ability to seduce women, is only an actor who expresses nothing. Complaining that he has to wear a mask depicting death, Skat states: 'Are the women going to like me in this getup? Will I make a hit? No! I feel as if I were dead already.'

When blacksmith Plog finds his wife Lisa, who, after running off with Skat, wants to get back with her husband, a very bad portrayal is made of the actor who manages to save himself from the wrath of the cuckolded husband with his theatrical skill by pretending to commit suicide. That ability is only a facade that can convince only simple-minded people, but not a refined and demanding audience that wants much more than what a handsome comedian can offer. And in fact Skat's empty talk and tricks do not work with Death.

Another detail of the film that reveals the presence of the director's personal experiences is the name of the knight's wife, Karin, which is the same as Bergman's mother with whom he had a problematic relationship. In this regard, it is important to note that the director recounts that when he was a child, his mother often rejected his affective impulses, something that he suffered greatly from (Karin Bergman later revealed to her son that she had behaved in this way on the advice of a pediatrician who had considered these behaviors harmful to Ingmar's development). Perhaps for this reason, the wife of Antonius Blok does welcome her husband, but does so rather coldly (the knight displays a similar behavior).

Some critics have expressed various hypotheses about the circumstance that neither the knight's wife nor the girl saved by Jöns appear in the Dance of Death seen by Jof at the end of the film. In my opinion, these are attempts to read too much between the lines and to attribute to *The Seventh Seal* meanings that are far from Bergman's intentions. First, one must correct those who have argued that there are no women in that vision, for Jof mentions Lisa, the blacksmith's wife. As for Karin, Jof had not met her and therefore could not recognize her. The girl's name is never mentioned and therefore how could Jof name her? Bergman therefore proved to be much more logical than the scholars of his film. We must also take into account a detail told by the director himself about the improvised way in which that scene was shot:

> The image of the Dance of Death beneath the dark cloud was achieved at hectic speed because most of the actors had finished for the day. Assistants, electricians, a make-up man and two summer visitors, who never knew what

it was all about, had to dress up in the costumes of those condemned to death. A camera with no sound was set up and the picture shot before the cloud dissolved.

The anachronisms and inconsistencies of the film and the references to the director's life made only professional historians frown. Despite not having the banal and predictable patterns of Hollywood films, *The Seventh Seal* follows the classic structure of plots that aim to please the average viewer (happy ending included), seasoning everything with a simple summary of Camus's thought that satisfies the most educated viewers and critics. The mixture turned out to be apt and the film had a good international success. As Bergman himself recounts, having gained the attention of a wide audience, critics, and producers with the award he received in 1956 at the Cannes Film Festival for *Smiles of a Summer Night*, he borrowed money from Bibi Andersson to go immediately to Cannes where he easily convinced the director of the Swedish Film Institute, elated by the large number of rights for *Smiles of a Summer Night* that he was selling, to finance the making of *The Seventh Seal*, which he had previously rejected. Despite the small budget and the few days in which it was shot, the time was ripe (Camus won the Nobel Prize for Literature in 1957) and the film 'swept like a forest fire across the world.' Perhaps it is true that with *The Seventh Seal* Bergman resolved his doubts about faith in God and his fear of death, but what is certain is that thanks to the success of that film he acquired the economic security and freedom in the artistic field whose lack had previously troubled his life.

8

WOMEN, BROTHERHOOD, EQUALITY, AND THE LAND OF OPPORTUNITY

Unlike the films examined in the previous pages, the movies analyzed in this final chapter are not strongly characterized by social or political themes. Nevertheless, some parts of these films were clearly influenced by contemporary ideals and issues, a particularity that warrants their inclusion in this book.

Strong and influential women

In the analysis of *Brother Sun, Sister Moon*, it has been pointed out that, in order to create a connection between the young reformers of the contemporary age and the characters of the film, the director included in his work various themes that were anachronistic for the Middle Ages, among which was the emphasis on the fact that women should have a relevant active role in society. *Brother Sun, Sister Moon* is probably the movie that most emphasizes this theme, but there were also other directors who followed a similar approach by showing historically incorrect examples of strong female characters—often made through the complete distortion of history—in order to adapt to the changing role of women in contemporary society and thus also to please the female audience.

In Italy, women's claims began to have a significant diffusion starting from the student protests of 1968, but the ground was made fertile by the deep economic and social changes which had occurred in the previous years. Suffice it to think of the improvement in the schooling of the population, the remarkable industrialization of a part of Italy, with the consequent loss of importance of agriculture and the increase in the population of the cities, the economic boom, and the diffusion of electrical appliances that greatly alleviated the work of many women, allowing them to dedicate themselves to other activities. Highly symbolic is the date, 1961—the beginning of a decade characterized by tumultuous transformations—in which an Italian film was released that presents a female character with some of

DOI: 10.4324/9781003153139-9

those characteristics. In *Rosmunda e Alboino* (*Rosmund and Alboin*), the director completely twisted how the King of the Lombards, Alboin, who invaded Italy around 568/569, was killed. According to the main medieval source of that episode, Paul the Deacon's *History of the Lombards*, Rosmund had her husband Alboin killed in revenge for the king's heinous act of forcing her to drink from a cup made from her father's skull. The murder was performed by Peredeus, a very strong warrior, who was obliged to execute it in the following way.

> As Peredeus would not give his consent to the queen when she advised so great a crime, she put herself at night in the bed of her dressing-maid with whom Peredeus was accustomed to have intercourse, and then Peredeus, coming in ignorance, lay with the queen. And when the wicked act was already accomplished and she asked him whom he thought her to be, and he named the name of his mistress that he thought she was, the queen added: 'It is in no way as you think, but I am Rosmund', she says, 'and surely now you have perpetrated such a deed, Peredeus, that either you must kill Alboin or he will slay you with his sword.'

In the film, the way Alboin was killed, i.e. through the weapons available to Rosmund, cunning and sex, is changed. It is in fact a handmaiden of the queen to perform that action by striking the king with a sword. In line with the spirit of the period in which the film was released, that woman thus demonstrated that she was capable of acting to obtain what she wanted without resorting to the expedients typical of the role traditionally attributed to women. The hypothesis that the medieval story was changed also because it contained particulars that censorship and the conservative press and audience could have considered as scandalous should not be ruled out. If this is what happened, the filmmaker caught two birds with one stone.

Brother Sun, Sister Moon is not the only film to depict Clare anachronistically. While not reaching Zeffirelli's excesses, in *Francesco* (1989) by Italian director Liliana Cavani we see Clare taking on a guiding role by gathering, after the saint's death, his old companions and remembering with them what Francis had accomplished. Not only did this episode never happen, but it goes against the fact that the real Clare spent her life in seclusion.

I have personally experienced that this narrative strategy works well with a female audience. The female students of my class on the Middle Ages in Italian films and novels have, in fact, displayed a great appreciation for the way Clare is portrayed in Zeffirelli's and Cavani's movies, while they have shown a strong sense of annoyance with her depiction in the film *I Fioretti di san Francesco* (*The Flowers of Saint Francis*, 1950), shot in a period when feminist claims were not yet relevant (the director Roberto Rossellini also followed the medieval sources much more than his colleagues). In *The Flowers of Saint Francis* Clare is only mentioned in a brief episode which is set at the time when she already entered the convent and is mostly depicted as a statue of the Virgin Mary, i.e. as a mute object to be venerated, which has nothing to do with a real woman.

In order to present a happy end to the film that would change the image of total defeat of the only female character in *The Name of the Rose* (1986) by J. Annaud, based on the homonymous novel, a fictional work, but set in a rather accurate historical framework, the young peasant girl, unjustly accused of being a witch, does not die at the stake as in the book, but is saved by some peasants. The latter even cause the death of the evil Dominican inquisitor Bernard Gui who hastily condemned the girl and two monks accused of being heretics to the stake. Besides not being present in the novel, this last episode never took place in the Middle Ages and Bernard Gui continued to try heretics and witches until his death, which occurred due to natural causes.

In the TV series *The Name of the Rose* (2019), Marguerite, the companion of the heretic Dolcinus, who in the book makes a brief appearance in the memories of one of his former followers, takes on the role of a modern and super active revolutionary. To soften the tragic but realistic tone of the novel and give further space to strong female characters, the TV series adds that a heretic managed to save the couple's daughter who grew up and developed a desire for revenge against the oppressors who had burned her parents at the stake. The torch of the fight was therefore not extinguished and it was a woman who carried it forward. Significant is a comment of the actress impersonating Marguerite because she takes for granted that what she has played is real History.

> Dolcinus and Marguerite were revolutionaries in the Middle Ages, and their story addresses issues that make people discuss and still resonate today, such as respect for others, tolerance, and gender differences.

In the TV series a patina of contemporaneity is also provided to the peasant girl who in the novel is accused of being a witch. She is in fact transformed into a war orphan and a refugee from southern France.

In other films there is no lack of female characters who anachronistically do not hesitate to wear heavy armor, take equally heavy weapons, and fight against warriors. Imitating 1930s women, who during the militarization of the Soviet Union were asked by propaganda to give their contribution in that field as well, in *Alexander Nevsky* we see a young woman from Novgorod so impressed by the incitement to face the German invaders that she follows the example of her fellow citizens by arming herself to the hilt and fighting the enemy in the final battle. Perhaps inspired by that film, in *The Great Warrior Skanderbeg* (1953), a Soviet-Albanian co-production recounting the exploits of the fifteenth-century Albanian leader Skanderbeg against the expansionism of the Turks, an Albanian woman also gives her contribution to the fight against the invaders by participating, arms in hand, in a charge of Albanian knights against the Turks. Unlike the Novgorod female warrior, however, she dies on the battlefield, thus emphasizing that women too paid with their blood for the freedom of their people.

Messing with history and legends, the director of *King Arthur* (2004) shows a Celtic woman, named Guinevere, first firmly resisting the violent attempts of a Christian bishop to convert her and, after being freed by the Roman officer Arthur, fighting at his side against the evil Saxon invaders. In Britannia, in the first century AD, that is, four centuries before a leader named Artorius clashed with the Saxons, a female leader is attested (Budica led a revolt against Roman rule), but it is not reported that she threw herself among the enemies, shooting arrows with her bow as Guinevere does in the film. In the medieval legends about King Arthur, Guinevere is the ruler's wife and stays in the palace while her husband fights and on one occasion creates serious problems by having an affair with Lancelot, Arthur's best knight and loyal friend.

Two Pictish female warriors, able to defeat all men (except, of course, the hero of the film), are also present in *Centurion* (2010), set during the attempt of the Romans to take over the land of the Picts (modern Scotland) at the beginning of the second century AD. In particular Etain stands out. She has an implacable hatred for the Romans guilty of having exterminated her family and of having raped her and cut out her tongue when she was a child. Noteworthy is the physiognomy of the main female characters in the film. Etain's distinctiveness is implicitly emphasized by her appearance, which is completely different from that of the other Picts (the actress playing her is Ukrainian; the other Pictish female warrior is a Belgian actress). The same thing is true for Arianne, a Pictish woman accused of being a witch by the chief of her people and for this reason forced to live alone, who does not give any importance to her ethnicity and first helps the Romans whom Etain is hunting and then falls in love with one of them. In this case the actress is an English blonde with a sweet and reassuring look.

Even the formidable female warrior that in *Dragon Blades* sows havoc among the enemies with her arrows is but one of the many inventions of the film. Relevant is the fact that this character is not Chinese as the hero of the film, but belongs to another people, i.e. a 'barbarian', with costumes different from those of the civilized Chinese. It is no coincidence that the hero's Chinese wife fights like her husband for a just cause, but she does so using the weapons of pedagogy, that is behaving as a civilized woman who follows the role assigned to her by the society to which she belongs. The combination of warrior woman and exotic physiognomy is found in *The Last Legion* (2007), where an unlikely female fighter from India helps the 'good guys' to free the young Roman Emperor Romulus Augustus from the hands of the barbarians.

As already pointed out, in *300* Queen Gorgo is the embodiment of the strong-willed woman, the ideal companion of a right-wing leader, who has sex by her own choice and finds pleasure in it, shows her husband the right path to take, is ready to sacrifice her body for the good of her spouse and the community, possesses remarkable oratorical skills and knows how to move men's minds, and, in case of need, does not hesitate to use weapons both to avenge a personal affront and to eliminate a dangerous traitor.

The equally invented female characters of *Barbarossa* display a behavior of free and determined women that has perhaps aroused some perplexity even among their peers at the beginning of the third millennium. Tessa refuses to marry the perfidious Barozzi, who has obtained her father's consent by paying, because she loves a brother of Albert of Giussano. After his death, she becomes a nun and, when Barozzi enters the monastery to take her, she prefers to commit suicide by throwing herself from the walls of the nunnery (the scene is obviously taken from *The Last of the Mohicans*). An even more independent and strong-willed spirit is shown by her sister, Albert's future wife, who is always ready to use a knife on anyone who dares to bother her, including Barozzi whom she almost killed, even though she knew that her attempt would have led her to certain death. Following the principle that even among the adversaries of the good guys there are characters with admirable qualities, in the film Barbarossa's wife always incites her husband when he has some doubts about his campaigns. Moreover, she displays such a proud leader's attitude in her harsh reprimand of the behavior of her husband's cousin who, instead of bringing soldiers and fighting alongside the sovereign, prefers to stay at home and provide only a financial contribution to the emperor's campaign, that the relative of Barbarossa says that Frederick should have been concerned about having a wife who acted and spoke like a man.

Thanks to the several films about Joan of Arc and the fact that this character interested filmmakers from the dawn of silent movies until recent times, we can examine how a female character changed over the course of nearly a century of adaptations. Probably concerned that the story of a girl who dressed as a man, had told a king what to do, and led an army of men could be poorly received by male spectators and conservative women and give her modern peers strange ideas (keep in mind that in 1917, the year the film was released, neither in the United States nor in Europe were women allowed to vote and serve in the army), director Cecil DeMille not only emphasized in the title of the film that Joan was a woman (*Joan the Woman*) but, in the opening caption, to the brief explanation of who this his-torical figure had been, he added that, despite everything she had done, she had essentially remained always a woman.

> It is founded on the life of Joan of Arc, the girl patriot who fought with men, was loved by men, and killed by men—yet retained the heart of a woman.

DeMille also never made his Joan wear men's clothes and even added a skirt over her armor. He, however, did not care that the actress chosen to play Joan of Arc, the opera diva Geraldine Farrar, had a strong build and some masculine features and could thus convey the idea that Joan of Arc acted like a man because she looked like a man. The director found that statement surprising when a journalist pointed it out to him.

In 1928, Carl Theodor Dreyer and Marco de Gastayne put things right both in the title of their films—*La Passion de Jeanne d'Arc* (*The Passion of Joan of Arc*) and *La merveilleuse vie de Jeanne d'Arc* (*The Wonderful Life of Joan of Arc*)—and in the appear-ance and clothing of their Joan. After all, DeMille's de-masculinization operation would have been a disaster in the different atmosphere of the 1920s that had con-tributed to some successes in women's emancipation. Between ups and downs, the process of women's rights continued in the following decades and therefore no director ever dared repeating what DeMille had done. In the films on Joan of Arc, however, the description of the behavior of the Maid of Orleans changed. Dreyer's depiction of Joan, whose face is often streaked with tears and is in great pain during the trial, is considered a masterpiece by critics but did not do well at the box office. That portrayal of Joan was never shown again in subsequent films, probably because it conveyed the image of a fragile woman that did not fit in with the status acquired by women during the twentieth century in the Western world.

It is no coincidence that in Luc Besson's 1999 blockbuster, *The Messenger*, Joan is depicted as a super-active and strong-willed female since childhood, who suffers with dignity the injustices and violence (including a rape during her imprisonment) committed against her by men. In an interview Milla Jovovich, the actress who played her in that film, stated that: 'Joan was really a mover and a shaker. She was a real Tasmanian devil', that is how many women of those years expected a female leader of their time to act. To be noted is the fact that in *The Messenger* the initial retraction that Joan did is described as the result of a sort of psychoanalytic session of the protagonist to whom appears a man challenging the genuineness of her actions. These particulars, along with the undeniable beauty and sensuality of the actress, a former model of Ukrainian origin, contributed to making that very expensive film a commercial success.

The fact that the real Joan was a teenager was omitted in most of the films about her. In addition to the desire to have an actress who could act (this was one of the reasons for the disaster of one of the two films in which a teenager was used), this particularity was probably also due to the fact that for the contemporary world it was hardly acceptable that a girl could play the role of a heroine of that magnitude.

In the contemporary world, however, there are various models of emancipated women that are different from the one traditionally attributed to women. There is no shortage of those who criticize the model of the strong-willed woman because in this way they copy male behaviors. Inspired by this debate and the belief that the world would be free of conflict if political leaders were women and not inspired by male models, in the TV series *Vikings* (2013–2020) the clash between the Vikings and the Indians is avoided because a Viking woman goes to parliament with the chief of the natives who is a woman. A precursor to the role of women bringing peace when men want war is found in Cecil DeMille's *The Crusades* (1935). Probably influenced by the achievements of women in the previous years and the desire of the US government to remain neutral in the international scenario at that time, the director assigned the wife of Richard the Lionhearted the role of peacemaker between the Christian king and Saladin.

Brotherhood and the fight against oppression

Since the second half of the eighteenth century, the events concerning Spartacus, the gladiator who between 73 and 71 BCE led the most dangerous slave revolt in Antiquity, have attracted the attention not only of historians, but also of politicians, activists, and novelists. Suffice it to say that Marx compared Garibaldi to Spartacus and that the leftist organization that promoted the Socialist revolution in Germany at the end of World War I was called the League of Spartacus. In the United States, during the Red Scare in the late 1940s and in the 1950s, Spartacus became the symbol of resistance to an oppressive system. Inspired by those ideals and atmosphere, Howard Fast (1914–2003) wrote a novel based on Spartacus. Due to the intervention of FBI director J. Edgar Hoover, Fast was placed on the lists of suspected Communists and all publishers rejected his book that he finally published at his own expense in 1951. At the end of McCarthyism, the US actor Kirk Douglas read it and was so impressed that he co-produced a film based on the novel (*Spartacus*, 1960) and played the protagonist.

In the case of the Spartacus of Antiquity we do not have sources that illustrate the point of view of the rebels, but we must remember that in the ancient world slavery was a system that characterized all societies, including Athens, the cradle of Western democracy. The fact, also present in the movie, that Spartacus and his companions rebelled against the Romans to create an egalitarian society without slaves is therefore historically inaccurate. They had undoubtedly taken up arms against their masters to free themselves from a terrible condition but, in all probability, once free they would have not hesitated to have slaves of their own. Regarding the most famous scene of the film—that is when, after having defeated the rebels, the Romans ask the prisoners to reveal which one of them is Spartacus, promising life to those providing the information, and the former gladiator denounces himself to save his companions, who, however, all together state to be Spartacus—it is an invention to highlight the solidarity that the oppressed of all ages should have shown among themselves even in the face of the danger of being condemned to a cruel death. Perhaps Fast hoped that this would also happen during the Red Scare in the United States, a hope that, as he himself witnessed, was mostly a pious illusion.

Equality and land for everybody and the dangers of not fulfilling these wishes

Four years after *Spartacus*, there was another film set in Antiquity (*The Fall of the Roman Empire* by Anthony Mann) strongly influenced by the clash between American progressives and conservatives and by the role that the United States had and wanted to assume towards the rest of the world. Suffice it to say that it was released in the midst of the struggle for civil rights for African Americans. In 1958, President Eisenhower had even sent the army to a city in the South of the United States where, going against the law on de-segregation of the schools, some African-American students had been denied access to a school. In those years numerous activists for civil rights and participants in demonstrations were severely beaten by the police and some of them were assassinated, probably by members of the Ku Klux Klan.

The election in 1959 as president of the United States of John Fitzgerald Kennedy, supporter of the 'New Frontier' project, which aimed to create a more equal society, generated great hopes among the supporters of those ideals. Hopes for a better world and for the implementation of non-aggressive policies by the United States were also raised by Kennedy's actions in foreign policy. In the fall of 1962 Kennedy was able to convince the Soviet Union to give up building a missile base in Cuba without intervening militarily. The Cuban missile crisis intensified diplomatic relations between the two superpowers and in 1963 they signed a treaty that placed a significant limit on nuclear testing.

Stressing that 'those who make peaceful revolution impossible make violent revolution inevitable', Kennedy presented a new role for the United States in Latin America by creating the Alliance for Progress, which aimed to support economic development and the defense of human rights in that area. In order to provide international social and economic assistance to developing countries and to present a better image of the United States in the world (often perceived as a devious colonizer), he established the volunteer program significantly called Peace Corps. One gesture that greatly propagated Kennedy's image as a champion of a better world was his visit to West Berlin on June 26, 1963, where he gave a speech criticizing the building of the wall that divided the city into two parts.

Although this had been Kennedy's main image, on several occasions he gave evidence of how the world of politics could corrupt those ideals. Concerned that the actions of the grassroots civil rights movement might cause him to lose the support of white Southern Democrats, he cooled his support for that movement considerably, provoking the anger of those groups who accused him of not keeping his campaign promises and of having used his support for their cause to be elected president. In the spring of 1961 Kennedy gave his consent to the attack against Cuba by some anti-Castro volunteers. When that attempt failed, he authorized Operation Mongoose during which thousands of sabotage actions were carried out against the Cuban economic infrastructure. During his administration, the number of American 'military advisors' in southern Vietnam also increased considerably.

Despite its title, *The Fall of the Roman Empire* does not describe the end of the Roman Empire, but the episode that, according to the director, caused the decline that led to its end. The movie begins with the Roman Emperor Marcus Aurelius (d. 180 AD) going to the northern frontier of the empire where his army is fighting some northern barbarians. The emperor wishes to promote equality among all his subjects regardless of their ethnic background and the color of their skin. His speech to the representatives of the peoples of the Roman Empire undoubtedly reflects the ideals and aspirations of the early 1960s: equal civil and political rights for all.

> You have come from the deserts of Egypt, from the mountains of Armenia, from the forests of Gaul, and the prairies of Spain. You do not resemble each other, nor do you wear the same clothes, nor sing the same songs, nor worship the same gods. Yet, like a mighty tree with green leaves and black roots, you are the unity which is Rome. Look about you and look at yourselves, and see the greatness of Rome. Two hundred years ago the Gauls were our fiercest enemies. Now we greet them as friends. In the whole world, only

two small frontiers are still hostile to us. One here in the north which separates us from those who are called barbarians. The other in the east, Persia.
Only on these two borders will you find walls, palisades, forts, and hatred.
But these are not the frontiers Rome wants. Rome wants and needs human
frontiers. We've had to fight long wars. Your burdens have been great. But
we come now to the end of the road. Here, within our reach, golden centuries of peace. A true Pax Romana (Roman Peace). Wherever you live,
whatever the color of your skin, when peace is achieved, it will bring to all,
'all', the supreme rights of Roman citizenship. . . . No longer provinces, or
colonies but Rome, Rome everywhere. A family of equal nations. That is
what lies ahead. May the Gods hasten the day.

The idealism of Marcus Aurelius is also directed towards the outside world, in particular to the relations he intends to establish with his enemies. In fact, he has this
significant dialogue with Livius, commander of the Roman troops engaged in fighting the barbarians, who promises to bring him soon the head of the enemies' leader.

MARCUS AURELIUS: No, Livius, please don't bring me his head. I wouldn't know
    what to do with it. Bring him to me alive.
LIVIUS: But he is the heart of the barbarians.
MARCUS AURELIUS: Then bring me the heart of the barbarians. I wish to speak
    with him. . . . It is time we find peaceful ways to live with those you call
    barbarians.

However, Marcus Aurelius is aware that without the right people such ideals will
never be realized and it is also possible that the situation could get worse. Knowing
his son Commodus, who together with his supporters aims to implement measures
opposite to his own, the emperor tells Livius that Commodus should not be his
successor. Marcus Aurelius therefore entrusts Livius with the task of fulfilling his
dream. He is, however, poisoned by some followers of Commodus who thus want
to secure important positions under the new emperor. The film had already been
shot when John Fitzgerald Kennedy was assassinated (November 22, 1963) and
it cannot be determined if any changes were made after that tragic event. Those
who saw the film in 1964 most likely noticed the similarities between the killing of
Marcus Aurelius and Kennedy's assassination and especially the fact that these two
statesmen had been eliminated to not allow them to carry out their idealistic plans.

On the other hand, the director certainly had in mind the dangers inherent in
the aggressive foreign policy of the United States, and especially what could happen
in the name of defending the so-called American way of life against the supposed
dangers of the spread of Communism. The debate in the Roman Senate between
those who want to implement some of Marcus Aurelius's projects (General Livius
and the wise Greek teacher Timonides) and Commodus's supporters, who are in
favor of an iron-fist policy against non-Romans, recalls what happened in the 1950s
and early 1960s. The proposal of Livius to settle the barbarian prisoners on unused

lands of the Roman Empire so that they could be put to good use and the empire could benefit from this and the bitter reaction of a supporter of Commodus who replies that the opponents of Rome should be treated without mercy, because that was the Roman way of dealing with them, recalls what occurred in 1954 in Central America. At that time the president of Guatemala, Jacobo Arbenz, a moderate and an opponent of the Communists, had proposed to confiscate unused land and distribute it to landless peasants. Some of that land was owned by the United Fruit Company whose investors included numerous American politicians, the Secretary of State John Foster Dulles, and the head of the CIA Allen Dulles, John's brother. The reaction of the United States was immediate. The CIA organized a coup in Guatemala, and Arbenz was deposed and forced to leave his country. The move radicalized many moderates in Latin America and greatly increased the hatred for the US. Noteworthy were, for example, the violent anti-US protests that broke out during Vice President Richard Nixon's 1958 tour of Latin America.

Timonides's speech constitutes a warning to Romans (and Americans of the 1960s) about the reactions that violent and aggressive policies can provoke and echoes the previously mentioned warning from Kennedy that 'those who make a peaceful revolution impossible make a violent revolution inevitable.' To prevent a disaster, it is necessary that the ancient Romans (and modern Americans) change their attitude towards these issues.

> I am a teacher, and as a teacher I know that when I have tried to teach the same lesson for a hundred times and still the pupil does not understand, then I am forced to the conclusion that perhaps there's something wrong, either with the lesson or with the teacher. A hundred times we have taught those we have called barbarians what it means to make war with Rome. We've burned their villages, we've crucified their leaders, we've enslaved their young. Fires go out, the dead are buried, the slaves die, slowly. But their hatred that we leave behind us never dies! Hatred means wars. Wars mean tribute torn from our provinces, taxes, hunger, disease. How costly that is! How wasteful! And yet the answer is simple. We must have no war. . . .
>
> Honorable Fathers, we have changed the world—can we not change ourselves?

The response to those words instead highlights the mentality of the most radical wing of American conservatives who considered those ideas as un-American nonsense that only newcomers and Jews (often associated by the American right in those years to supporters of Communism) could formulate. Because none of the screenwriters were born in the US, two of them had a Jewish background and one of them was blacklisted during the McCarthy Era, those references were certainly made on purpose.

> No war? When your friends continually attack us. This is treason! These people have proved their aims very clearly. To destroy us and to destroy the whole Roman way of life. . . .

Equality . . . Freedom . . . Peace. Who is it that uses these words but Greeks, and Jews, and slaves. Behind him and his people are the Vandals, untold millions of them, waiting for a moment of weakness, ready to destroy us. If we take these barbarians in amongst us, our enemies will say is it because we are weak.

When the Senate votes in favor of the proposal of the supporters of Marcus Aurelius's ideals, one of the latter states: 'Now can we say to our Senate, to our empire, to the whole world, look! Here we meet in friendship, the blond people from the North and the dark people from the South. What we have done here could be done the whole world over.' In this case, too, the movie clearly addresses contemporary problems such as the integration between whites and blacks rather than describing the past.

The film quickly takes a pessimistic turn correctly predicting the disasters that occurred in the 1960s and the 1970s both within the United States with the fierce struggles for civil rights (just think of the assassinations of Robert Kennedy and Martin Luther King Jr. and the violent riots that erupted following the murder of the latter) and outside (war in Vietnam).

Upon becoming the new emperor, Commodus dismantles all the measures implemented by Marcus Aurelius, whom he considered to be a weak ruler. The barbarians, transformed into peaceful and productive farmers, are massacred by order of Commodus. It is true that Livius, notwithstanding the incredible cruelty of Commodus, rebels against him and kills him. Yet he refuses to become the new emperor (he declares that if he accepted it he would have executed all the Roman politicians, thus going against the ideals he wanted to realize) and retires to private life, while the senators fight for control of the empire. A voice-over adds that this was the beginning of the end of the Roman Empire, an allusion to the fact that this could also be the beginning of the end of the American Empire. After all, in his acceptance speech Kennedy made this warning:

We stand today on the edge of a New Frontier—the frontier of the 1960s, the frontier of unknown opportunities and perils, the frontier of unfilled hopes and unfilled threats.

Inclusion and coexistence

In the analysis of *300*, the presence of racist messages regarding people from Sub-Saharan Africa has been highlighted, proving how those prejudices and stereotypes were still present at the beginning of the twenty-first century. In the United States and in some European countries, however, the long and often painful history of the process for the full inclusion of blacks in society and of the attitude toward them has not been exclusively characterized by rejection and racism. In fact, there has been no shortage of white people, especially those with leftist views, who have helped to ensure that things changed. The desire to make people with Sub-Saharan African origin feel part of the Western world and to show positive attitudes towards them has influenced some directors of films set in Antiquity and the Middle Ages, lead-ing them to include in their works characters with that physiognomy. The ideals behind such a choice are certainly meritorious, but such a decision has resulted in situations that are historically highly improbable and sometimes completely wrong.

At the beginning of *Kingdom of Heaven*, to highlight the open-mindedness and positive attitude toward 'the other' of Godfrey of Ibelin (one of the good guys in the film), among the warriors in his service there is one who clearly has the physi-ognomy of a sub-Saharan African. It is not completely impossible that there were slaves in the Kingdom of Jerusalem in the twelfth century who had that origin, but it is highly unlikely that they could fill that role. In the context of that film, it is relevant that a black man is in the entourage of a 'good' Christian and not in that of a 'bad' Christian. Similar considerations apply to the character with a sub-Saharan physiognomy who, in *The Last Legion*, is in the retinue of the good Roman general who rescues the last western Roman emperor (a young boy) from the cruel barbarians. In *Centurion*, a sub-Saharan African is among the small group of brave legionaries who survive the ambush of the Picts and risk their lives to free their commander. In his case, the director adds the classic patch that is worse than the hole he intends to repair. Neglecting the particular that the region called Numidia was north of the Sahara, that character claims to be Numidian.

FIGURE 8.1 The 'Numidian' (screenshot from *Centurion*)

More relevant roles were assigned to Afro-American actors in two films about Robin Hood shot in particular periods. At the beginning of the 1990s, as if to mark the end of the previous decade politically dominated by the Republicans, in *Robin Hood: Prince of Thieves* (1991) Morgan Freeman is Azeem, an Islamic believer who escapes from a Near East Muslim prison with Robin, played by the liberal actor Kevin Costner. He travels to England with the latter and helps him in his fight against the evil sheriff of Nottingham. The role of the character played by Morgan Freeman was developed even more unrealistically in *Robin Hood*, released in 2018, that is, in the midst of the presidency of Donald Trump, distinguished by racially motivated statements, and the 'Black Lives Matter' movement. In the film, African-American actor Jamie Foxx plays the part of John, who both instills in Robin the will to fight against the wicked and trains him (image 8.2). It should also remembered that an actor from Sub-Saharan Africa plays a quite relevant role in *King Arthur: Legend of the Sword* (2017).

Fanciful ideals of peaceful coexistence among people of different religious faiths and multiculturalism, clearly created to appease Italian audience and to promote the idea of the positive historical role played by many Italians in the Mediterranean and the Near East, are instead present in the mini-series for Italian television *I Crociati* (*The Crusaders*, 2001), also available as a film with subtitles in various languages.

FIGURE 8.2   Robin and John (screenshot from *Robin Hood*)

Produced on the occasion of the one thousandth anniversary of the conquest of Jerusalem in 1099 by Western Christians, the TV series recounts the adventures of three young men from Aurocastro, a small town in Southern Italy, who, wishing to leave behind the conditions in which they found themselves, join the expedition to take the Holy City. Born from a Christian woman impregnated by a Muslim pirate, Peter was raised by a learned bell maker (whose sound recalls joy and peace) who taught him to read and write in several languages. Treated as an outcast by the other inhabitants because of his origins, Peter must also suffer the humiliation of not being able to marry his beloved Mary, whose father wants to give her in marriage to a rich warrior. Mary's brother, Andrew, instead refuses his destiny as a miller, while Richard, the son of a nobleman, decides to leave to escape his uncle who killed his father and took away his lands.

During the crusade, the three young men are the only ones who do not participate in the looting and indiscriminate acts of violence of the other crusaders, who come from other parts of Europe, and who also target Jews in order to obtain loot. The three young men are also rewarded with a sweet happy ending. Although Richard is unable to stop the massacre of the population after the fall of Jerusalem and is killed in the course of the violence, he has nevertheless found his faith and becomes an eternal symbol of peace and knowledge. In fact, Peter places him anonymously in a tomb in Aurocastro and states that this pilgrim had come there 'to bring peace to others and light to us all.' Having achieved his desire to be an honorable warrior, Andrew becomes the lord of Aurocastro and marries Rachel, a Jewess he had saved from the crusaders. Back home, Peter is able to fulfill his dream of marrying Mary, who had refused to marry a rich and detestable warrior, and takes the place of his adoptive father, thus becoming a valued member of his community.

No information is given as to how all this had been possible. Christians and Jews could not marry. Had the fervent Jewish Rachel converted? Or had she pretended to do so, thus running the risk of being executed? And how is it possible that the 'bastard' Peter could be accepted by the community after having always been treated as an outcast? None of these characters are obviously based on medieval sources. In the case of Peter we have an example that is the opposite of what is described in the movie. According to some medieval texts, in the tenth/eleventh century lived Saint John Terista, who was the son of a Christian and a Muslim from Sicily. Raised in the Christian faith by his mother, he was so opposed by his father and other Muslims that he decided to leave Sicily and become a monk in Calabria. The improbable idealism of *The Crusaders* and the tragic events following the attacks on the Twin Towers on September 11, 2001, caused both the TV series and the film to be unsuccessful and soon fell into oblivion.

Land of opportunity

The director of *Kingdom of Heaven* is the British director Ridley Scott, but this very expensive movie was produced by a film company in the United States where most of its intended audience resides. Scott therefore did not fail to employ narrative strategies aimed at creating analogies between the past and the present that would suit the mentality of Americans for whom the frontier and the self-made man are among the most relevant founding myths of their nation. It is no coincidence that at the beginning of the film, when Godfrey describes the Kingdom of Jerusalem to Balian, he portrays it as a world where what counts is not a person's social background but what he or she is worth.

> Do you know what lies in the Holy Land? A new world. A man who, in France, had not a house is, in the Holy Land, the master of a city. He who was the master of a city begs in the gutter. There, at the end of the world, you are not what you were born but what you have it in yourself to be.

A hint to this particularity of the Kingdom of Jerusalem with an explicit reference to the difference between Europe and the 'New World' appears even before the film begins. Among the captions aiming at contextualizing the historical period there is the significant statement that 'Europe suffers in the grip of repression and poverty. Peasant and lord alike flee to the Holy Land in search of fortune and salvation.'

Balian himself insists on this theme. Ironizing on the difference between Europe and the 'Kingdom of Heaven', he claims that in France a few yards of silk is enough to be a nobleman. The super-bad and arrogant French nobleman Guy of Lusignan reiterates this point by refusing to sit at the king's table with Balian, because he is an illegitimate son, and reminding everyone that 'in France this would not inherit. Here there are no civilized rules.' The wonderful particularity of that world, devoid of social rules and conventions even in emotional relationships, is highlighted by another of the film's 'good' characters. Explaining to Balian why she is attracted to him, Sybilla tells him: 'I'm here because, because in the East between one person and another there is only light.'

Balian embodies the ideal of the self-made-man. Thanks to his skills, he makes the most of the opportunity he is given and from being an illegitimate son and a humble blacksmith in a remote French village, he turns into a hero capable of effectively facing Saladin, saving many people, winning the heart of a queen, and, not to be overlooked, enhancing the poor possessions he inherited from his father (thus improving the conditions of those who live there). On that occasion he also proves to be a hard worker who has no problem in getting his hands dirty and working together with his employees.

Scott himself confirmed the analogy between the United States and the Kingdom of Jerusalem, stating in an interview that 'the knight was the cowboy of that era. He carried with him degrees of fairness, faith and chivalry.' Again, the past is depicted through a 'contemporary' lens with which the director portrays that world. After the seizure of Jerusalem in 1099, some Europeans were able to improve their social standing, but before long the new kingdom became one of the most hierarchical societies ever created in the Middle Ages. As already pointed out, the so-called Crusades were a pilgrimage in arms. Like all pilgrims, the Western Christians who participated in the campaigns perceived them as a vow and after fulfilling it they returned home. Few of them remained in the Holy Land, which, unlike contemporary America, was never a land to which a part of the European poorer classes migrated.

FILMOGRAPHY

Alexander Nevsky (1938), directed by S. Eisenstein.
Barbarossa (2009), directed by R. Martinelli.
The Black Knight (1954), directed T. Garnett.
Braveheart (1995), directed by M. Gibson.
Brother Sun, Sister Moon (1972), directed by F. Zeffirelli.
Burebista (1980), directed by G. Vitanidis.
The Canterbury Tales (1972), directed by P. Pasolini.
Centurion (2010), directed by N. Marshall.
La Chanson de Roland (*The Song of Roland*, 1978), directed by F. Cassenti.
El Cid (1961), directed by A. Mann.
Columna (1968), directed by M. Drăgan.
I Crociati (*The Crusaders*, 2001), directed by D. Othenin-Girard.
The Crusades (1935), directed by C. DeMille.
Dacii (1967), directed by S. Nicolaescu.
The Decameron (1971), directed by P. Pasolini.
Ettore Fieramosca (1938), directed by A. Blasetti.
The Fall of the Roman Empire (1964), directed by A. Mann.
I Fioretti di san Francesco (*The Flowers of Saint Francis*, 1950), directed by R. Rossellini.
The Flower of the One Thousand and One Nights (1974), directed by P. Pasolini.
Francesco (1989), directed by L. Cavani.
The Great Warrior Skanderberg (1953), directed by S. Yutkevich.
Die Hermannschlacht (*The Battle of Hermann*, 1924), directed by L. König.
Joan the Woman (1917), directed by C. DeMille.
King Arthur (2004), directed by A. Fuqua.
King Arthur: Legend of the Sword (2017), directed by G. Ritchie.
Kingdom of Heaven (2005), directed by R. Scott.
Kryzact (also known as *Knights of the Teutonic Order*, 1960), directed by A. Ford.
The Last Legion (2007), directed by D. Lefler.
La merveilleuse vie de Jeanne d'Arc (*The Wonderful Life of Joan of Arc*, 1928), directed by M. de
   Gastayne.

The Messenger (1999), directed L. Besson.

Mihai Viteazul (*Michael the Brave*), also known as *Last Crusade*, (1971), directed by S. Nicolaescu.

La Nave (*The Ship*, 1912), directed by E. Bencivenga.

La Nave (*The Ship*, 1921), directed by Gabriellino D'Annunzio and M. Roncoroni.

The Name of the Rose (1986), directed by J. Annaud.

The Name of the Rose (2019), TV Series, directed by G. Battiato.

El Naser Salah el Dine (*Saladin the Victorious*, 1963), directed by Y. G. Chahine.

The Patriot (2000), directed by R. Emmerich.

La Passion de Jeanne d'Arc (*The Passion of Joan of Arc*, 1928), directed by C. T. Dreyer.

Robin Hood (2018), directed by O. Bathurst.

Robin and Marian (1976), directed by R. Lester.

Robin Hood: Prince of Thieves (1991), directed by K. Reynolds.

The Seventh Seal (1957), directed by I. Bergman.

Spartacus (1960), directed by S. Kubrick.

Ştefan cel Mare-Vaslui 1475 (*Stephen the Great—Vaslui 1475*) (1974), directed by M. Drăgan.

300 (2007), directed by Z. Snyder.

Tiān Jiàng Xióng Shī (*Celestial General, Heroic Army*, also known as *Dragon Blade*, 2015), directed by D. Lee.

Vikings (2013–2020), TV series created by M. Hirst.

Vlad Ţepeş (*Vlad the Impaler*, 1978), directed by D. Năstase.

BIBLIOGRAPHY

Primary sources

Arab Historians of the Crusades, selected and translated from the Arabic sources by F. Gabrieli. Translated from the Italian by E. J. Costello (Abingdon, 2010).

The Decameron of Giovanni Boccaccio, translated by J. M. Rigg (London, 1903).

Francis of Assisi: Early Documents, volume I, eds. R. J. Armstrong-J. A. W. Hellmann-W. J. Short (New York, 1999).

Historia Roderici, in *The World of El Cid: Chronicles of the Spanish Reconquest*, translated and annotated by S. Barton and R. Fletcher (Manchester, 2000), pp. 90–147.

The History of Herodotus, translated by G. Rawlinson (London, 1858–1860).

The Legend of Saint Clare (1254–1255), in *Clare of Assisi: Early Documents*, edited and translated by R. J. Armstrong (Saint Bonaventure, New York, 1993), pp. 246–308.

The Rare and Excellent History of Saladin, or, al-Nawādir al-Sultaniyya wa'l-Mahasin al-Yusufiyya, by Bahā' al-Dīn ibn Shaddād, translated by D. S. Richards (Aldershot, 2001).

Thomas of Celano, *First and Second Lives of Saint Francis*, translated by David Burr, available in https://sourcebooks.fordham.edu/source/stfran-lives.asp (accessed on September 22, 2021).

Secondary works

Most of this book is based on my own analysis of the movies. I have cited the secondary sources from which I have drawn the information mentioned in this volume.

1: *Invaders and heroes*

Die Hermannschlacht (*The Battle of Hermann*):
M. M. Winkle, *Arminius the Liberator: Myth and Ideology* (Oxford, 2016), pp. 127–58.

Alexander Nevsky; *El Cid*; *Kryzact* (also known as *Knights of the Teutonic Order*):
J. Aberth, *A Knight at the Movies: Medieval History on Film* (London-New York, 2003), pp. 107–47.

2: *Inspiring models of unity, independence, and identity*

Burebista; *Columna*; *Dacii*; *Mihai Viteazul* (*Michael the Brave*); *Ştefan cel Mare-Vaslui 1475* (*Stephen the Great-Vaslui 1475*); *Vlad Ţepeş* (*Vlad the Impaler*):

O. Colăcel, *The Romanian Cinema of Nationalism: Historical Films as Propaganda and Spectacle* (Jefferson, 2018), chapters 4–5.

Barbarossa:

T. di Carpegna Falconieri, 'Barbarossa e la Lega Nord: A proposito di un film, delle storie e della Storia', *Quaderni storici*, 132 (2009), pp. 859–78.

Braveheart:

T. Edensor, *National Identity, Popular Culture and Everyday Life* (Oxford-New York, 2002), chapter 5.

C. McArthur, *Brigadoon, Braveheart and the Scots: Distortions of Scotland in Hollywood Cinema* (London-New York, 2003), chapters 5, 8.

3: *Leftist social and political topics in 1960s and 1970s movies*

La Chanson de Roland (The Song of Roland):

J.-P. Bertin-Maghit, 'Trois cinéastes en quëte de l'historie. Entretien avec René Allio, Frank Cassenti et Bertrand Tavernier', *Image et son: Revue de cinéma*, 352 (1980), pp. 108–17.

H. Desrues, 'La Chanson de Roland. Entretien avec Frank Cassenti', *Image et son: Revue de cinéma*, 328 (1978), pp. 15–19.

J.-P. Oudart, 'Le P.C.F. et la mode rétro: La Chanson de Roland', *Cahiers du cinéma*, 295 (1978), pp. 50–51.

L. Ramey, ' "La Geste que Turoldus declinet": History and Authorship in Frank Cassenti's Chanson de Roland', in *Hollywood in the Holy Land: Essays on Film Depictions of the Crusades and Christian-Muslim Clashes*, eds. N. Haydock-E. L Risden (Jefferson, 2009), pp. 147–60.

The Canterbury Tales:

Pasolini's statements about Chaucer and Boccaccio can be found in http://www.centros tudipierpaolopasolinicasarsa.it/approfondimenti/appunti-su-i-racconti-di-canterbury-di-pier-paolo-pasolini/ (accessed on March 22, 2021).

4: *Video right-wing agendas*

La Nave (*The Ship*):

M. Bernabò, *Ossessioni bizantine e cultura artistica in Italia. Tra D'Annunzio, fascismo e dopoguerra* (Naples, 2003), pp. 26–35, 38.

5: *Medieval Muslims and Christians, and modern agendas for the Middle East*

J. Aberth, *A Knight at the Movies: Medieval History on Film* (London-New York, 2003), pp. 91–106.

P. B. Sturtevant, 'SaladiNasser: Nasser's Political Crusade in El Naser Salah Ad-Din', in *Hollywood in the Holy Land: Essays on Film Depictions of the Crusades and Christian-Muslim Clashes*, eds. N. Haydock–E. L Risden (Jefferson, 2009), pp. 123–46.

7: *The Black Death, existentialism, old and new fears, and private matters*

J. Aberth, *A Knight at the Movies: Medieval History on Film* (London–New York, 2003), pp. 216–43.

I. Bergman, *Images: My Life in Film* (New York, 1994).

I. Bergman, *The Magic Lantern: An Autobiography* (London, 1988).

The English translation of the screenplay of *The Seventh Seal* can be found in I. Bergman, *Four Screenplays* (New York, 1960).

The English translation of Cecco Angiolieri's poem is taken from https://publishing.cdlib.org/ucpressebooks/view?docId=ft4870069m&chunk.id=d0e6243&toc.depth=1&toc.id=d0e5911&brand=ucpress (accessed on September 22, 2021).

8: *Women, brotherhood, equality, and the land of opportunity*

Movies about Joan of Arc:

J. Aberth, *A Knight at the Movies: Medieval History on Film* (London–New York, 2003), pp. 278–98.

The comment of the actress impersonating Marguerite in the TV series *The Name of the Rose* can be found at https://www.iodonna.it/spettacoli/tv/foto-racconto/tutto-su-il-nome-della-rosa-dal-libro-di-eco-al-film-alla-serie-con-john-turturro/?img=10 (accessed on March 8, 2021).

The Fall of the Roman Empire:

P. W. Rose, 'The Politics of *The Fall of the Roman Empire*', in *The Fall of the Roman Empire: Film and History*, ed. M. M. Winkler (Malden–Oxford, 2009), pp. 241–61.

MAPS

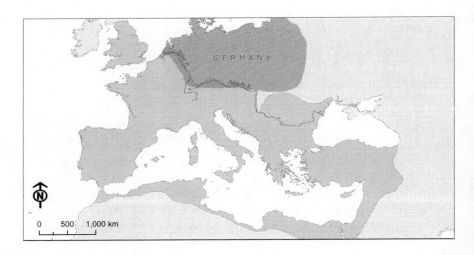

MAP 9.1   The Roman Empire and Ancient Germany

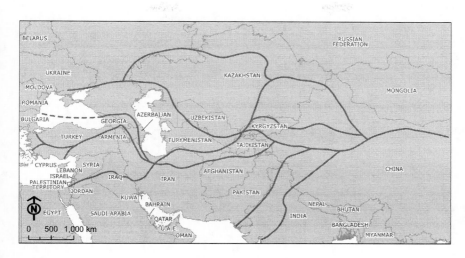

MAP 9.2   Silk Roads with modern countries

MAP 9.3   Modern Eastern Europe

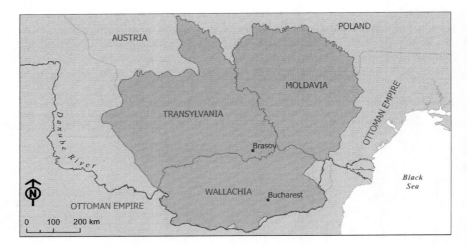

MAP 9.4   The main regions of late medieval and early modern Romania

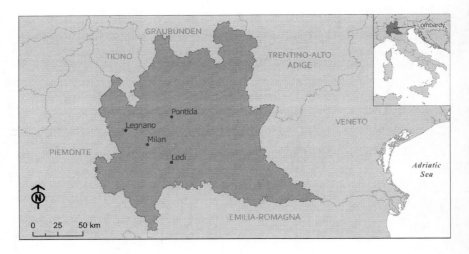

MAP 9.5   Lombardy

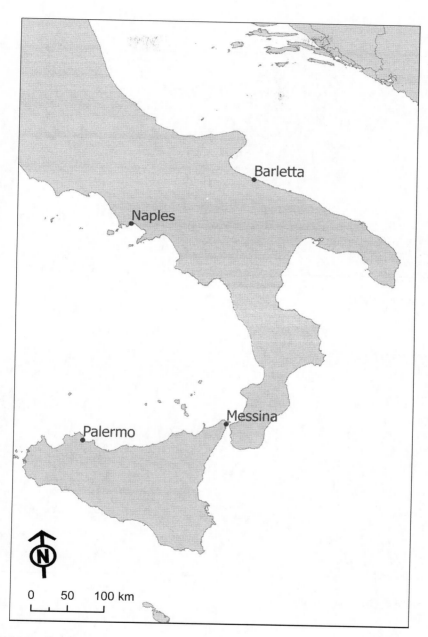

MAP 9.6   Southern Italy

MAP 9.7 Spain

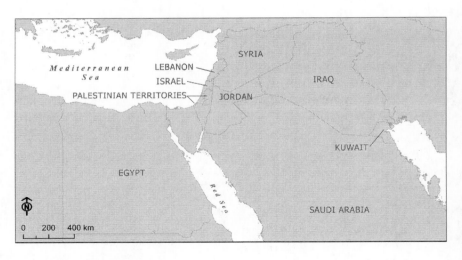

MAP 9.8 Modern Middle East

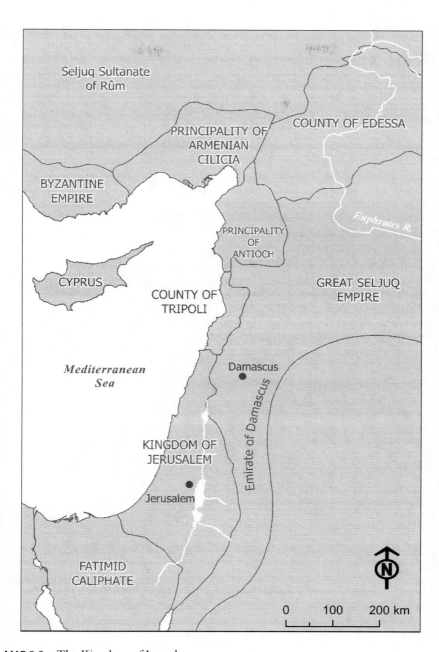

MAP 9.9   The Kingdom of Jerusalem

INDEX